Orange

KIRAN

Made with ❤ on the Notion Press Platform

www.notionpress.com

"How many times have people used a pen or paintbrush because they couldn't pull the trigger?"

— Virginia Woolf

The Beginning

"So, this is how love feels like..." Kyle murmured, the words lingering in the air as he stared up at the ceiling. The book he had been reading lay on his chest, its pages now closed, the story still echoing in his mind. The soft, warm glow of the evening sunlight bathed the room, spilling across the floor and casting long, lazy shadows that seemed to deepen the emotional weight of the moment. With a quiet sigh, he let his thoughts wander, feeling the lingering effect of the story as the light slowly faded around him.

The stillness of his room felt amplified by the slow, rhythmic ticking of a distant clock, as if the entire world had settled down with him in this moment. He closed his eyes, letting himself drift, his mind returning to scenes from the story, each one vivid and colored by the warm evening glow that seeped through his window. Slowly, the line between reality and dreams blurred, the quiet wonder he felt carrying him gently into sleep. The morning sunlight crept into Kyle's room. He elicited, blinking as he woke up, and noticed a single tear at the corner of his eye. It was strange—he couldn't remember what he'd dreamed about, but something had clearly stirred his emotions. Brushing it off, he headed to the kitchen, where his mom was setting out breakfast, a comforting routine he never took for granted.

As he sat down, his mom gave him a warm smile. “You look like you slept well,” she said, pouring him a cup of tea. Kyle returned her smile, reaching for his plate. “Yeah. I hope I can sleep like that every night.” He glanced at the food and sighed contentedly. “And I could get used to breakfasts like this too.”

His mom laughed, patting him on the shoulder. “Good news, then—your dad’s coming today. He wanted me to tell you that you can invite your friends over for dinner if you’d like.” Kyle’s eyes lit up.

“That sounds great! They’d love that.” He took another bite, savoring the flavors, and glanced up with a smile. “Thanks, Mom.”

“Anytime, sweetheart. Just don’t make a habit of missing breakfast here,” she teased, clearing his empty plate. Kyle chuckled, standing up and grabbing his keys. “No chance of that happening.” He leaned over, giving her a quick hug. “Bye, Mom. See you tonight!”

“Have a good day, Kyle!” she called as he walked out.

Outside, his retro cruiser waited in the driveway, gleaming in the morning light. Though the bike was an old model, Kyle had poured a lot of time and care into modifying it to suit his own style. He’d swapped the original handlebars for a low-rise pair that gave him a more streamlined grip, added a custom leather seat, and upgraded the exhaust to give it a deep, throaty growl. With a turn of the key, it came to life, the engine settling into a steady, low rumble. He loved the feeling of it under him, the bike's power and unique look a small reflection of his own quiet confidence.

As he rode through Orange, he took in the beauty of the morning, where familiar houses and shops stood framed by greenery. The small town was tranquil, its streets lined with old oaks and cobblestone paths leading to places everyone knew by heart. The smell of fresh oranges occasionally wafted in from the groves nearby, a reminder of the town's famed sweets. Every face he passed seemed familiar, a nod or wave exchanged without thought—Orange was just that kind of town. Small, connected, a place where everyone seemed to know everyone else. The ride up to the university was a pleasant ascent, the campus located on a low hill that overlooked the town. The university itself was an impressive mix of old-world charm and modernity. Tall stone archways framed the entrance, leading to sprawling courtyards filled with benches shaded by trees that were older than the students themselves. Ivy crawled up the older brick buildings, while newer glass structures mirrored the greenery around them, blending the two eras seamlessly.

Kyle pulled into the parking lot and cut the engine, enjoying the brief silence before the familiar purr of another bike broke it. Sam pulled up beside him, his arrival punctuated with a playful smack to the back of Kyle's head.

"Sup, idiot. Did you find it?" Sam greeted, his tone

Kyle rolled his eyes, turning to give Sam a look. "There are better questions to ask first thing in the morning." Sam just smirked, leaning in closer. "Come on, spill. I'm not dropping this." Kyle shrugged, glancing away as he tucked his keys into his pocket. "Later," he said, deflecting with a small grin that he knew would keep Sam guessing for a while. The two of them made their way up the steps, joining the steady stream of students heading inside. The hallways were alive with energy, posters for the upcoming cultural events tacked on every available surface. The annual festival was around the corner, and the university was buzzing with anticipation. Colorful flyers advertised everything from music and dance competitions to science fairs and debates, each one promising a showcase of the university's diverse talents. As they weaved through the crowd, a voice called out from across the hall, "Hey, you guys planning on winning this year too?"

Kyle gave a modest smile, but Sam raised a fist with a confident grin. "You already know it!" he shot back, his voice carrying just enough swagger to earn a few laughs and nods of agreement from other students.

Kyle shook his head, chuckling at Sam's unshakable confidence. Despite Sam's cockiness, the team had earned their reputation for being a tough group to beat. They were known around campus not just for their competitive spirit but also for their camaraderie—a rare mix that kept them close and everyone else on their toes.

As they reached their classroom just before the bell rang, Kyle took his usual seat by the window while Sam sat behind him. Kyle glanced over his shoulder, noticing Sam scanning the room.

"Where are they?" Kyle asked, keeping his voice low as the professor entered the room. Sam shrugged. "No idea. But they should be here soon."

Just then, the sound of footsteps echoed down the hallway, growing louder until three familiar figures rushed through the door. The professor glanced at his watch, mildly annoyed. "Come on, but try to be on time next time." The three quickly settled around Sam and Kyle in the last row. Kyle and Sam leaned over and asked in unison, "Where were you guys?"

Ryan spoke up first, running a hand through his hair. "My bike had some issues this morning, so I called Nate to come pick me up."

Everyone then looked at Ryder, who laughed, raising his hands in mock surrender. "Woke up late," he admitted with a shrug. The group shared an exasperated look, unsurprised by Ryder's response. He was always on his own time, and they'd all come to expect it. As the class dragged on, Nate tapped Kyle's and Sam's shoulders. "So... any plans for tomorrow?" Ryan nodded. "I need to fix up my bike. Shouldn't take long, but I'd welcome the company." Kyle offered a small nod, saying, "I'll tag along." Ryder chimed in, "No plans here. I'm good for whatever." Kyle looked over at Sam. "So, the usual spot?"

The group nodded, all agreeing. Kyle added, "My mom said my dad's coming home tonight, and she invited everyone for dinner. We'll spend the night there and head out Saturday evening." With a satisfied look, he leaned back, the weekend already shaping up to be one of those perfect times with his friends.

As the morning classes finally dragged to a close, everyone eagerly awaited the lunch bell, tapping their feet or glancing at the clock every few minutes. When the bell finally rang, Ryder was the first to jump up, stretching with a sigh. "So, what's for lunch today?" Ryder asked, his eyes lighting up as he glanced around at his friends. "Chinese, I think," Ryan replied. The group agreed with a few nods, gathering their things as they made their way to the cafeteria to pick up their lunch parcels.

Lunch in hand, they headed outside, following a path that curved around the university grounds. Built atop a small hill, the university had a mix of classic and modern architecture that blended effortlessly, with old stone buildings side-by-side with sleek glass structures. The view from the back was stunning, overlooking the entire town of Orange, nestled in a sea of green treetops and winding streets.

They made their way to their favorite spot—a secluded, open patch behind the school grounds where students technically weren't allowed without supervision. It had a perfect view over the edge of the hill, looking out over Orange with its cozy streets, familiar faces, and the famous orange-scented air.

As they sat down, unpacking their food, they began eating and chatting, laughing over inside jokes and sharing stories from the morning. After lunch, as they were heading back toward the main campus, a familiar voice echoed across the grounds.

"You guys don't listen, do you? You're not supposed to hang out there," called Mr. Peterson, their usually lenient history professor, who had caught them here more than once.

The group exchanged amused glancces before walking over, with Sam taking the lead. He reached into his pocket, pulling out an apple, and handed it to Mr. Peterson with a hopeful grin. "For your trouble, sir," he said, barely containing his laughter.

Peterson tried to keep a straight face, his lips twitching with amusement as he looked down at the apple. Before he could respond, Nate pulled a small toy from his bag and held it out. "And for Tracy," he added, smiling as he watched the professor's surprise. Kyle added, "It's tracy's birthday today, isn't it, Mr. Peterson?" Peterson raised an eyebrow. "How did you know?"

"We know everything," Ryder quipped, smirking. They all burst into laughter, and even Peterson couldn't hold back a chuckle. "Alright, you troublemakers. Just get back to class." He shook his head as they sauntered off, chatting as they headed down the hall. Once out of earshot, Ryan turned to Kyle with a curious smile. "So, how did you know it was Tracy's birthday?" Kyle shrugged, his eyes twinkling. "Overheard him talking on the phone yesterday." Everyone laughed again, giving Kyle a light shove or a playful punch as they walked back to class, their footsteps echoing in the hall. It was these small, unexpected moments that seemed to bond them, making the ordinary feel a little more memorable. The final class of the day stretched on, the minutes ticking by as the sunlight began to cast long shadows across the room. Kyle stared out the window, his mind half on the lesson and half on the weekend plans that awaited. When the bell finally rang, signaling the end of the day, the group exchanged eager glances, already knowing what came next.

They made their way to the locker room to change for football practice, the familiar smell of worn leather and liniment filling the air. They each grabbed their gear and changed quickly, lacing up their cleats with a sense of purpose. Sam, always the loudest, strode out onto the field with a swagger, tossing a ball from hand to hand as he turned to the others. "No competition can match us," he announced, his voice carrying over the field with an air of absolute confidence.

Nate rolled his eyes, sharing a look with Ryan. "Let's hope that confidence doesn't backfire on us someday," he said, smirking. Ryan nodded in agreement, crossing his arms. "Yeah, one of these days, Sam, you're gonna jinx it for us."

Sam grinned, unfazed by their teasing. "Just trust the process, fellas," he replied, gesturing around the field with a sweeping arm. "Champions are born right here."

Ryder gave Sam a friendly shove. "If only you put that confidence into your passing game." The group laughed, settling into the easy rhythm of their banter before practice officially began. They ran drills, passing and shooting, the sound of cleats tearing into grass filling the air as they pushed each other to improve. Nate's strategic mind kicked into high gear, calling out plays and pointing out gaps in the formation. Kyle, who wasn't the loudest but had a knack for reading the game, positioned himself just right, often anticipating his friends' movements before they made them.

After an intense hour, they gathered at the edge of the field, catching their breath as the sun dipped lower, casting the field in warm orange light. They looked at one another, sweaty and tired but with grins stretching from ear to ear. This—this was the feeling they chased, the sense of Rapport and shared purpose that made every practice, every game, worth it.

As they gathered their things and began heading off the field, Sam threw his arm around Kyle's shoulders. "Alright, genius. Where to now?" Kyle smiled, shrugging as he wiped the sweat from his brow. "Think we could all use a cold drink after that."
"Drinks it is," Ryan chimed in, nodding enthusiastically as they headed back to the locker room, already planning their next move. The day might have been over, but for them, the night was just beginning.

After a quick shower and change, the group packed up their bags, the exhaustion of the day settling over them like a comfortable weight. They headed down to the parking area, where their bikes stood in a row, ready to take them into the calm night. Ryan hopped on behind Nate, and with a nod to each other, the four bikes roared to life, their engines filling the quiet evening with a low, rumbling growl. The descent down the hill was peaceful, a stark contrast to the energy of practice, as they rode in silence. Each of them was wrapped in their own thoughts, letting the cool night air and the familiar sound of their bikes create a steady, comforting rhythm. It was one of those nights where words weren't needed—just the presence of friends was enough.

As they coasted down the winding hill, the scenery shifted from the open expanse surrounding the university to the cozy, familiar streets of Orange. The night had settled in fully, casting the town in a soft, moonlit glow, and the lights of homes and street lamps twinkled against the rich green backdrop of trees that bordered the town. Orange at night had a quiet charm all its own. By day, the town was full of friendly faces and lively greetings, but at night it transformed, becoming tranquil and almost otherworldly. The gentle hum of their bikes was the only sound that echoed down the empty streets, where the shadows of large oaks and orange trees stretched across the quiet lanes, their leaves rustling softly in the night breeze.

As they approached the town's center, the warm, nostalgic scent of orange sweets filled the air. It was a subtle sweetness that wafted from the local candy shop, open late enough that the aroma became a fixture in the night air. There was something about this town at night that felt timeless, as if nothing here had changed in years—and yet, the possibilities of tomorrow seemed just within reach.

They arrived at a small snack shop at the edge of town, a spot they'd been frequenting since high school. The shopkeeper, an older man with a warm smile, waved them over, clearly happy to see them. They each grabbed a cool drink from the counter, murmuring a few greetings as they made their way back outside to sit on their parked bikes. The night was quiet, and they took long gulps from their bottles, relishing the refreshing coldness after a long, hard day.

As the silence stretched, Kyle was the first to break it, looking down at his bottle thoughtfully. "You ever feel like you need... a change? Like, something different? I'm just so bored of the same routine." The group exchanged glances, each of them caught by surprise at Kyle's words. Nate was the first to respond, a curious expression crossing his face. "What do you mean?" Kyle shrugged, fiddling with the bottle cap. "I don't know... just something new. Something that makes life feel... less predictable." Nate nodded, and after a pause, he changed the subject, asking, "So, any thoughts on what extra classes you're all signing up for next week?" Ryder was quick to answer, stretching his legs out in front of him. "Probably business studies. You know, something I can actually use someday." Nate nodded in agreement. "Same here. Makes sense."

Ryan leaned back on his bike, cracking a small smile. "Computer course for me. Figured it wouldn't hurt to get some tech skills."

"Management for me," Sam chimed in, his tone confident. "Might as well get the upper hand."

Then all eyes turned to Kyle, who seemed to hesitate before he answered. "I think... I'll go with Arts & Music, maybe." The group fell silent again, processing the mix of their choices. It was a small decision, but somehow it felt like the start of something different. They sat there quietly, each of them sipping on their drinks and wondering what the future held, a sense of both familiarity and excitement settling over them.

Okay, let's go!" Sam declared, finishing his drink with a satisfied gulp. The group mounted their bikes and rode through the familiar streets of Orange, excitement buzzing in the air as they made their way to Kyle's home. Kyle's house was a charming two-story structure, painted a soft shade of yellow that seemed to radiate warmth. Nestled among vibrant flowerbeds and leafy trees, it exuded a welcoming charm that matched the town's cozy atmosphere. The porch, adorned with hanging ferns, was a favorite spot for Kyle to relax and read on warm evenings.

They parked their bikes in the garage, the sound of engines quieting down as they dismounted. The moment they stepped inside, the mouthwatering aroma of freshly cooked dinner enveloped them, making their stomachs growl in anticipation.

Kyle! You're home!" his mother called from the kitchen, her voice warm and inviting. She was busy arranging plates at the dinner table, her apron dusted with flour, a sign of her recent culinary efforts.

"Hey, Mom! Smells amazing!" Kyle replied, a smile spreading across his face as he walked in.

“Go get freshened up,” she instructed, pointing toward the hallway. “Dinner will be ready soon.”

The boys nodded and headed toward the bathroom, chattering amongst themselves. One by one, they hopped into the shower, the sound of water mingling with their banter. As they emerged, each feeling rejuvenated and ready for a hearty meal, they gathered at the dinner table, the enticing smell of food still hanging in the air. While waiting for the last of them to finish, Kyle’s mom chatted with the boys, asking about their classes and teasing them about their football practice. “So, have you guys figured out who’s going to win the tournament this year?” she asked, her eyes sparkling with mischief.

Sam beamed, leaning back in his chair. “Us, of course! No one can compete with our skills, right, Kyle?”

“Absolutely,” Kyle said with a chuckle, “But I think we might need to practice a bit harder!”

Just then, the front door swung open, and Daniel, Kyle’s dad, stepped in, a broad smile lighting up his face. “I’m back!” he announced, holding several packages in his arms. “And I come bearing gifts!”

The boys leaned forward with interest as Daniel set the packages down on the table. “I got something for

each of you," he said, his eyes twinkling with excitement. He began handing out the gifts, and as they tore into the wrapping, leather jackets emerged, each embossed with their names in elegant script. "Wow! This is awesome!" Ryan exclaimed, trying his jacket on immediately. The others followed suit, admiring their new jackets in the light of the dining room. "Thanks, Mr. Thompson! This is so cool," Nate said, beaming with appreciation.
"Yeah, thanks, Mr. T!" Sam added, giving a thumbs-up.

Daniel chuckled, settling down at the table, pleased with their reactions. "You guys deserve it. Now, let's dig in! I hope you're hungry because your mother has outdone herself tonight." With laughter and lively conversation, they began to serve themselves, the dinner table transforming into a hub of camaraderie, shared stories, and the warmth of friendship that made Kyle's house feel like a second home. The evening stretched on with good food and even better company, and Kyle felt grateful to have such amazing friends by his side.

As the plates began to empty and the laughter quieted down, Daniel leaned back in his chair with a thoughtful look. "Boys, do you know why our town is named Orange?" he asked, catching everyone by surprise. The boys looked at each other, puzzled. They exchanged glances, realizing none of them had ever questioned the origin of the town's name. Daniel chuckled at their expressions and began to explain. “Well, the first orange tree in the country actually grew right here in our town. It was that simple, really. But over time, that original spot was left untouched, and the rest of the town was built around it.”

Their eyes widened, surprised by this discovery. “We’ve passed that spot so many times and never knew,” Nate murmured, still wrapping his head around it. Daniel smiled, pleased with their interest. “It was different back then—quieter, with orchards everywhere. My friends and I used to sneak off to that very tree sometimes after school, pretending we were explorers,” he added, a nostalgic gleam in his eye. The boys listened intently as he shared a few more stories from his childhood, memories of long summer days, harmless mischief, and the adventures he had with his own friends. The table grew quiet, each of them lost in thought, picturing the town they knew from a new angle. When the last bites were taken, the boys thanked Daniel and Kyle’s mom for the meal, their voices warm with appreciation. “Thanks so much, Mrs. Thompson—dinner was amazing,” Ryan said, and the others nodded in agreement.

Kyle gathered a few of the plates to help clear the table. “You guys go on up,” he told his friends. “I’ll be right behind you.” The boys made their way upstairs to Kyle’s room, still talking about the stories Daniel had shared, as Kyle lingered in the kitchen a moment longer, smiling to himself. Tonight, his home felt fuller than ever with the energy of their friendship and the stories they were making together.

They shuffled into Kyle's room, a cozy sanctuary filled with warmth and character. The walls were painted a soft shade of blue, giving the space a calm ambiance. Posters of fantasy landscapes and famous literary quotes adorned the walls, evidence of his love for reading and art. A small bookshelf stood in one corner, its shelves filled with well-worn novels and poetry collections, each spine a testament to his passion for literature.

The bed was neatly made, with a quilt that Kyle's grandmother had gifted him, its vibrant patterns adding a splash of color to the room. On the bed, a single book lay open, pages slightly curled at the edges.

It was the same collection of quotes and poetry Kyle had immersed himself in the night before. Nate picked it up, glancing over the lines. "Figures," he murmured, a smile tugging at his lips. "Definitely seems like something he would read." He set the book down on the desk, where it nestled among a few scattered sheets of paper filled with Kyle's doodles and half-finished poems.

In addition to the book, Nate noticed an old sketchbook beside it. The cover was worn and the corners dog-eared, but as he opened it, he was taken aback by the stunning illustrations that filled each page. Landscapes bursting with life, portraits that seemed to capture emotions perfectly—each drawing showcased Kyle's remarkable talent and creativity. He couldn't help but admire the attention to detail and the passion that seemed to radiate from the artwork.

Just then, Kyle entered the room, holding something behind his back, a mischievous smile on his face. Before he could say anything, Sam, always the instigator, spotted an old tape recorder perched on the edge of the desk. With a quick press of the play button, the room filled with a familiar voice—Kyle's voice—attempting to sing, but without any rhythm or melody. It sounded more like someone reading a story than performing a song.

As the unexpected sound echoed around the room, the boys turned, stifling laughter as they looked at Kyle, who stood there with his head down, a hint of embarrassment creeping into his cheeks. The playfulness of the moment enveloped them. "Let's... let's not talk about that," Kyle mumbled, scratching the back of his head. "I thought I'd give singing a shot, but judging by your faces, I'm pretty sure that's my first and last attempt."

"Oh, definitely. You'd be doing a great service to society by sparing us," Ryder teased, still chuckling, his laughter infectious. They all burst into laughter, The sound of their joy echoed off the walls, mixing with the fading notes of Kyle's recording. Kyle couldn't help but laugh along with them, feeling a wave of comfort and belonging

Kyle, eager to shift the topic away from his singing mishap, brightened as he pulled a book from behind his back. "Here you go, Sam," he said, a hint of excitement in his voice. "And to answer the question you were so curious about this morning—I found it!"

Sam's eyes lit up; curiosity piqued as Kyle handed over the book. The cover was plain, but there was a certain charm about it. "You've been busy these last few days, huh?" he said, flipping it open. The title caught his attention: "Orange." He read it aloud, the name resonating with the town they all called home.

As they flipped through the pages, they noticed an unfortunate detail: the majority of them were blank, only a few scrawled lines filled the first few pages. "What's with the empty pages?" Nate asked, brows furrowing in confusion. Kyle shrugged, a shy smile creeping onto his face. "I wanted to write a story about our town," he explained, his voice soft but filled with passion. "But I want it to be interesting. I'll continue writing when something inspires me." The boys took a moment to read what was written. The initial pages reflected bits of his life—small moments, fleeting thoughts, and observations about Orange. Ryder smirked, unable to resist a quip. “Might as well just write a diary, Kyle,” he teased.

Kyle chuckled, shaking his head. “I would, but some things are better when they're not real,” he replied, his tone light but with a hint of seriousness. He took the book back from them, gently placing it in the cabinet beside his bed, a protective gesture as if he was safeguarding a piece of himself. The laughter faded as a comfortable silence settled in the room, the boys exchanging glances that conveyed understanding. They all knew that while Kyle's heart was in his writing, the journey to find his story would take time. The chatter carried on for another hour, worn out from practice, finally drifted off to sleep.

Morning arrived with soft light filling the room, and after freshening up, Sam, Nate, and Ryder gathered their things, saying they'd meet Kyle and Ryan at their usual spot around 5 p.m. Kyle and Ryan made their way to the kitchen, greeted by the smell of breakfast. Mrs. Thompson looked up with a warm smile as they sat down. As they started eating, she glanced at Ryan. “When are your parents going to be home?” she asked. Ryan smiled, replying, “They'll be back tomorrow evening.” Mrs. Thompson nodded, looking at him with motherly warmth. “Well, if you ever need anything, feel free to come by, Ryan.”

Ryan smiled back; his gratitude evident. "Thanks, Mrs. Thompson. You've done so much already. It really means a lot." After finishing up, Kyle stood and stretched, giving Ryan a nod. "Ready to check out your bike?" They both said goodbye to Mrs. Thompson and headed outside, hopping onto Kyle's bike. The gentle morning sun cast a warm glow as they rode through the streets, weaving between familiar corners of town and passing the quiet houses that lined the roads.

After a while, Ryan broke the silence. "So, what was that talk last night about you needing a change?" His tone was light, but there was a hint of curiosity beneath it.

Kyle exhaled, glancing over. "My life feels...stuck," he said, almost laughing at himself. "Like it's just going forward without actually going anywhere. Everything feels too routine, too predictable." Ryan chuckled, leaning back. "Man, some people dream about having stability like that. No surprises, no stress."

Kyle nodded, thinking it over. "Yeah, maybe. But it's not for me. I don't want to look back someday and feel like I just went through the motions, you know?" Ryan nodded, understanding Kyle's restlessness. They continued down the road in comfortable silence, each lost in thought as they approached Ryan's place, ready to tackle the day ahead. After the quiet ride, they finally reached Ryan's house. Ryan's place was a modest, single-story home with a welcoming charm, painted in a soft shade of blue. A small front garden, carefully tended by his mom, featured a mix of flowers and herbs, adding a touch of life and color to the cozy setting. They parked Kyle's bike at the end of the driveway, the morning sun casting a gentle glow over the porch where a few potted plants sat, giving the entrance a homey touch.

Ryan led Kyle toward the garage, pushing open the door to reveal a neatly organized space filled with tools, spare parts, and a few old knick-knacks. A workbench ran along one side, complete with a pegboard of tools hanging on the wall behind it. Just as they stepped inside, a sleek gray tabby cat slinked over, rubbing against their legs and purring softly.

"Hey, Bella," Kyle murmured, bending down to greet the cat with a gentle stroke. Bella responded with an affectionate head-butt, weaving around Kyle's legs before wandering off to find a sunny spot by the window.

Ryan grabbed a toolbox from the workbench. "Alright, let's get this done." They both crouched down by the bike, examining the damage. The busted chain was the first issue they spotted, along with a few other minor but fixable problems. Fortunately, Ryan had a spare chain stashed in the garage, and they got to work. Carefully, they took turns with the tools, methodically working through each issue, and after about two hours, the repairs were complete. Kyle watched with a hopeful grin as Ryan gave the bike a kickstart, and the engine roared to life.

Satisfied, Ryan wiped his hands on a cloth and glanced at Kyle. “Feel like grabbing some snacks?” he offered, gesturing toward the house with a smile. As they step inside Ryan’s house, Kyle sighs with relief. “A drink would be perfect right now,” They cleaned themselves up and headed to the kitchen. Ryan started rummaging through the cabinets, while Kyle leans casually against the counter, crossing his arms and glancing around the room. The kitchen had a cozy feel to it, with a small bowl of cat food on the table and a few photos on the fridge, one of which catches Kyle’s eye. “Your brother’s grown up a lot since last time I saw him,” Kyle notes, pointing at a picture of Ryan’s younger brother from his last soccer tournament.
“Yeah, he’s practically glued to that soccer field these days,” Ryan says, laughing. “Coach says he’s got potential, and he’s actually starting to believe it.”

Kyle grins. “Guess he’s taking after his big brother. Just wait, he’ll be beating you on the field in no time”. Ryan rolls his eyes. “Let him try. He’s good, but he’s got a long way to go before he catches up to me. The other day, he challenged me to a one-on-one, thinking he could outsmart me.”
“Oh, that must’ve been fun to watch,” Kyle chuckles. “Let me guess, you didn’t go easy on him?”

"Not a chance," Ryan says, smirking. "I gave him a taste of his own medicine. He's quick, though. Kid actually almost scored a couple of times."

Kyle grabs a bag of nachos off the counter and tosses it toward Ryan. "Keep training him, and one day, he'll give you a run for your money." Ryan laughs, opening the bag. "That's the plan. Who knows? Maybe he'll go pro someday." He pops a nacho in his mouth, then pauses thoughtfully. "It's weird, though. Feels like yesterday he was just a kid running around annoying the hell out of me."

"Time flies, huh?" Kyle says, pouring them each a glass of Coke. "One minute you're trying to get him off your back, and the next, he's practically following in your footsteps." They share a laugh, then settle into a comfortable silence, munching on their snacks. Ryan leans back against the counter, glancing over at Kyle. "Hey, thanks for helping me with the bike. I'd still be staring at that busted chain if it weren't for you."

"Anytime," Kyle replies, raising his glass in a casual toast. "Besides, I can't have my riding partner stranded, can I?" With snacks packed up for later, they lock up the house, grab two small bags of snacks, and head out to the garage, ready for the rest of their day.

Kyle and Ryan loaded up on their own bikes and began the ride out of town, the wind brushing past as they took in the clear afternoon. It was around 3 pm, and both felt the anticipation of reaching their favorite spot at the edge of town. Along the way, the two decided to take a quick detour to a small restaurant nestled on a roadside, known for its hearty meals and cozy, rustic feel.

As they pulled into the lot, Ryan stretched and laughed. "We're eating way more today than usual. Must be the miles adding up."

"Or maybe you're finally building muscle," Kyle teased, locking his bike as they headed inside. They grabbed a booth near the window, settling into their meals with a relaxed comfort only close friends shared. With each bite, they tossed around casual updates, talked about the last football practice, and made guesses about what kind of snacks the others would bring to the spot.

When they finished, they made their way back outside. Kyle glanced up at the darkening clouds. "Hey, looks like we might have rain on our hands." Ryan, always one to see the fun in a challenge. "Think we can outrun it?" Kyle raised an eyebrow. "You do realize you're on a bike, not a jet, right?"

They got back on their bikes, picking up speed as they headed toward the edge of town. The spot they were going to was tucked away on the far side of the hill that stretched across town and beyond. It was the same hill their university stood on, yet the other end held a special kind of magic: the view over the valley, with the sun setting on one side and the town lights flickering to life below. As they approached the familiar stretch, Ryan broke the comfortable silence. "By the way, did you hear about those new transfers? Apparently, they're joining the football team."

"Yeah?" Kyle responded, intrigued. "You sound more interested in the competition than the people."
Ryan laughed, nudging his bike forward. "Hey, it doesn't hurt to hope some of them are good-looking, does it?"
"Whatever helps your game man," Kyle shot back, shaking his head.

Just then, a soft drizzle began, misting the road in a fine spray. It was enough to make the air feel cool, the scent of rain mixing with the earth and the greens lining the road. The two picked up their pace, laughing as droplets started hitting their helmets and jackets. "Think this will clear up, or are we just gonna show up drenched?" Ryan asked.

"Guess we'll find out soon enough," Kyle replied, eyes ahead as the familiar contours of the hill came into view, their favorite spot just around the bend.
As Kyle and Ryan approached their favorite spot, the outline of the tree house appeared at the edge of the

hill, surrounded by the rich greenery and soft mist from the recent drizzle. Three bikes were already parked outside, their handlebars glistening with droplets. The tree house itself was a rustic charm—partially built into the large tree, sturdy and weathered, yet with an air of warmth that held years of memories. The view from here stretched far over the town and beyond, and today, the landscape was particularly stunning, the clouds casting a moody, shifting light over everything.

They parked their bikes beside the others, and as they turned, they spotted Sam a little distance away by the edge of the clearing, gripping rocks and hurling them into the distance, as if testing his strength. Kyle called out, "Trying to set a new record, Sam?"

Sam smirked, looking over his shoulder. "Just making sure none of you can out-throw me. Someone's gotta keep the competition alive!" He tossed another rock, watching it disappear into the grass, then trotted back over, slinging his arms around both Kyle and Ryan.

"So," he said, grinning, "what did you bring for us? Better be good." Inside, Ryder was sitting on an overturned crate, his hands moving in rhythm as he tried to perfect a new beatboxing pattern, humming under his breath as he played around with different sounds. Nate was crouched by the old cabinet, tinkering with the loose hinges. He barely looked up as Kyle and Ryan walked in but muttered, “Guess you guys finally made it, huh?”

“Only took us a scenic route,” Ryan replied, playfully rolling his eyes as he set down his bag. “Here you go, snacks galore!” He opened the bag to reveal the stash: bags of chips, packets of cookies, and even a few bottles of soda.

“Now, that’s what I’m talking about,” Ryder said, grabbing a pack of chips. “Beatboxing makes a guy hungry; you know?” They each grabbed something, settling into their usual places in the cozy interior. The tree house held everything that connected them: photos of their past hangouts tacked onto the walls, shelves lined with helmets, jackets, and random bike parts they’d collected over time. The faint smell of wood mixed with a hint of motor oil lingered, reminding them of their endless summers spent fixing up bikes or planning road trips they’d never quite taken.

Kyle wandered over to the photo wall, brushing his fingers across a particularly goofy picture of them from last year’s camping trip. “Remember when we got stuck in that rainstorm?” “Hey, it was a bonding experience!” Sam declared, taking a big swig of soda. “And besides, who else would sit in a leaky tent for hours just for the laughs?”

“True,” Nate chimed in, straightening up after securing the cabinet door. “But maybe next time, we pick a spot that doesn’t double as a swamp.” Everyone laughed, each one recalling their own version of that memory. As they munched on the snacks, the light from outside poured in through the small windows, illuminating the warmth and familiarity of their little retreat. Here, with their laughs echoing off the walls and the air thick with nostalgia, they felt like no matter how much changed around them, this place—and these friendships—would remain constant. The rest of the night at the tree house felt like a scene out of one of their favorite movies—everyone sprawled out on the old, comfortable couches and blankets they’d collected over the years, passing around snacks and watching a mix of action flicks and comedy classics. Between movie scenes, they talked about the upcoming term, a mix of excitement and curiosity in the air.

“So, we’re actually splitting up for a class this year,” Nate said, adjusting his glasses and looking around with a hint of surprise. “Can’t remember the last time we weren’t all together for cvcrything.”

“Yeah, but maybe that’s a good thing,” Ryder said, tossing a chip into his mouth. “Gotta expand a bit. Meet new people, make new... connections.” He wiggled his eyebrows, and Sam rolled his eyes. “Connections, huh?” Sam smirked. “Or you mean more girls to annoy?”
“Hey,” Ryder protested, laughing. “I’m just being

social." Kyle chuckled and shook his head. "Maybe it'll be fun, though. Mixing things up, seeing each other from different perspectives... like, who knows, maybe we'll all end up experts in totally different fields."

"Yeah, I'm definitely not studying computer science with you guys," Ryan joked. "But hey, maybe I'll pick up something that'll help us plan cooler trips." Soon their conversation shifted to the new students transferring in this year. They tossed around wild guesses, debating how many would be interesting or athletic, and whether any might actually pose some competition on the football field.

As the movies played on, they started to grow quieter, one by one drifting off into light sleep. Nate was the first to knock out, slumped against a pile of cushions, with Ryder following soon after, snoring softly. Kyle and Ryan stayed up a bit longer, chatting in hushed voices about their hopes for the year, before finally succumbing to sleep as well. The sounds of the tree house settled into the quiet hum of dawn, with only the faint breeze rustling through the branches.

The next morning, sunlight crept through the tree house windows, gently waking them. Yawning and stretching, they each packed up, taking turns groggily saying their goodbyes. They headed back to their homes to catch a few more hours of sleep and rest up for Monday. The weekend passed faster than they realized, and by Sunday evening, the usual rhythm of the town was returning, each of them readying for the week ahead. Kyle woke up with an unusual burst of excitement humming through him. It was the first day of their new courses, and he couldn't shake the thrill of starting fresh and meeting the new faces around campus. After a quick stretch, he showered, got dressed, and headed downstairs, feeling more awake than usual. His mom was already in the kitchen, setting the table with a warm smile. She looked up as he walked in, noticing his energized mood. "Well, someone looks happy this morning."

Kyle smiled as he sat down, reaching for a piece of toast. "I guess I am. Today's the start of something different, you know? I've been waiting to try out this art class. I mean, I always liked poetry, quotes & music, but I'm excited to really get into it."

His mom chuckled, pouring him a glass of juice. "Just don't go quoting books to everyone on the first day, alright? You don't want them thinking you're some mysterious, dramatic artist or something." She gave him a playful nudge. Kyle laughed, shaking his head. "Don't worry, Mom. I'll keep the dramatic quotes for later." He quickly finished his breakfast, making sure to savor it—he always appreciated his mom's cooking, but today it tasted especially good, maybe because he felt ready for anything. Standing up, he grabbed his keys from the side table, swung his bag over his shoulder, and kissed his mom goodbye.

"See you tonight, Mom!"

"Have a great day, honey. And don't forget—you're more than good enough, just be yourself," she added, giving him a reassuring smile as he headed out the door.

Kyle made his way to the garage, where his bike waited. He ran a hand over it, appreciating the familiar hum and power it gave as he started it up. The morning sun had just begun warming the streets, casting a golden glow over the sleepy town as he rode out, already seeing clusters of students heading toward the university. He felt a thrill as he neared campus, the building standing tall against the early sky. With the prospect of new classes, new people, and new experiences ahead, today already felt like the beginning of something big.

Kyle arrived at the university, spotting his friends by the bike stands, each of them looking as eager as he felt. As he walked up, Sam waved him over with a big grin, calling out, "Well, look who finally rolled out of bed!"

"Hey, it's not that late," Kyle shot back. "You guys just couldn't wait to see me, huh?"

"Of course not, man," Sam replied, giving Kyle a playful punch on the arm. "We're here for the new classes and new people. But hey, you're a close second."

Nate adjusted his glasses, a small but excited smile creeping onto his face. "I can't blame him. I mean, come on—finally, some fresh faces, maybe some real conversation starters."

"Ah, there it is," Ryder teased, leaning back against his bike. "Nate's just stoked for all the science clubs he can drag us to." Nate rolled his eyes, shrugging off Ryder's joke. "Laugh all you want, Ryder, but we both know you're itching to start 'networking' with all those business students." He made air quotes, and everyone laughed.

"Can't knock the hustle," Ryder replied with a wink, clearly unbothered. "Besides, I'm just prepping for my first million." Ryan grinned and leaned over, nudging Kyle. "How about you, Picasso? Ready to charm everyone in arts class? Gonna hit 'em with a Shakespeare quote or two?"

Kyle shook his head, laughing. "Yeah, I'll save the sonnets for later. Really, I'm just hoping it's as interesting as it sounds."

"Anything's better than last semester's lineup," Sam said, groaning. "I mean, remember history class? I could practically hear myself getting bored."

As they headed to their morning classes, the anticipation buzzed between them. They couldn't help counting down the hours to lunch, just waiting for the new courses to begin. When the lunch bell finally rang, they made their way to their usual location behind the campus. The chatter flowed easily as they ate, trading jokes, making guesses about who'd be in their classes, and even betting on who'd make the worst first impression.

As they wrapped up lunch, Kyle looked around. "Alright, so we're still meeting up at football practice to swap stories, right?"

"Obviously," Sam said, leaning back and stretching his arms behind his head. "I mean, who else is gonna tell you guys what really went down?"

"Yeah, like you're not the one we expect with a story anyway," Ryder replied, smirking. "I'm calling it now—Sam's coming back with some conspiracy theory about his professor." Sam put a hand to his heart, faking offense. "Hey! Just because I'm interesting doesn't mean I go looking for trouble."

"Oh, you attract it naturally," Nate added with a chuckle. With their plan set, they exchanged waves and friendly shoves before heading to their respective classrooms. The morning's jokes lingered, and as each one made their way into the unknown territory of new courses, there was a mix of excitement, nerves, and curiosity about the stories they'd bring back to each other. As Kyle parted ways with his friends, excitement bubbled up inside him, mingling with a hint of nervousness. The morning had been filled with lively conversations and anticipation, and now he was ready

to embrace something new. Climbing the stairs to the top floor, he focused on the rhythm of his footsteps, a quiet moment to gather his thoughts. Reaching the notice board, he leaned in, scanning the list of students enrolled in his art class. "Twenty students... not too many," he murmured to himself, a small sense of relief washing over him. With a smaller group, perhaps he'd have a chance to really connect with others. He noted the classroom location—top floor, facing the football grounds. Perfect spot, he thought, his spirits lifting further.
With purpose in his stride, he approached the classroom door, adjusting his shirt and giving his hair a quick ruffle, wanting to look at least somewhat presentable for his new classmates. He pushed open the door and stepped inside, greeted by an expanse of quiet and bright light streaming through the tall windows. The room was empty, the desks arranged neatly in rows, and he was the first to arrive. It felt inviting, the air tinged with the faint scent of fresh paint and clean paper.

He walked over to a cozy seat—the last desk by the window. It offered a view of the lush green football grounds below, where he could already envision the players warming up. He could see the goalposts standing tall, and the anticipation of the games ahead filled him with a sense of nostalgia. I wonder if I could kick a ball up to here, he thought, chuckling at the absurdity of the idea.

Kyle wanted to make an impression, he took a step toward the door, peering out to check if anyone was about to enter the classroom. The hallway was still empty, the sound of distant footsteps echoing down the corridor. Satisfied, he turned back to the classroom, a flicker of determination igniting within him.

With that in mind, he walked over to the whiteboard and grabbed a dry-erase marker. He paused for a moment, pondering what to write, wanting something that would set the right tone for his own journey in this class. Finally, he confidently wrote, "One Day or Day One," at the top of the board. He let the words linger for a moment, feeling a small thrill at the motivational touch he had added to the room.

With a satisfied smile, he returned the marker to its place and settled back into his seat, feeling the energy in the room shift slightly as he claimed his spot. The solitude was comforting, a moment just for him. As he looked out the window, the sun shone brightly on the football field, illuminating the grassy expanse where he and his friends had shared countless afternoons.

The silence wrapped around him, but it was a peaceful silence, one filled with promise. Kyle's thoughts drifted to his friends and the adventures they would share, wondering about their own classes and what stories they'd bring to football practice later. For now, he felt ready for whatever this new chapter held, taking a deep breath as he embraced the possibilities that lay ahead. One by one, students began to trickle into the classroom, their footsteps echoing lightly on the wooden floor. The air filled with the sound of zippers being pulled, books being opened, and the rustling of art supplies as everyone prepared for the class. The name of this course was Arts & music, and as Kyle surveyed the room, he realized it was a melting pot of creativity; students brought in not just their sketchbooks and paints, but also guitars, notepads filled with lyrics, and even a couple of ukuleles.

Kyle noticed some familiar faces among the crowd, but he only exchanged polite nods with them, still feeling a bit reserved in this new environment. He watched as a girl with brightly colored hair set up a small easel at the front, while a guy with headphones draped around his neck was fiddling with his guitar, tuning it with a focused expression. The buzz of chatter filled the room, interspersed with laughter and the occasional strum of an instrument.

As the students settled into their seats, Kyle took a quick count and noticed that two students were still missing. He glanced toward the door, hoping to see them appear, but just as he did, the teacher stepped into the room, her energy instantly lighting up the atmosphere. She had an infectious excitement that seemed to envelop everyone.

"Good morning, everyone!" she exclaimed, her voice warm and welcoming. She placed her belongings on the podium, a colorful array of art supplies, and looked around the classroom, her eyes sparkling with enthusiasm. "I'm Mrs. Arya, and I'm thrilled to be your guide through this journey of creativity! I want to hear from each of you, so let's start with introductions. Tell us your name, what inspires you, and what creative outlet you enjoy the most!"

Kyle felt a mix of nerves and anticipation, his heart racing at the thought of sharing something personal with the class. As the students began to introduce themselves, each one sharing a snippet of their passions and aspirations, he found himself getting more excited. He listened intently, trying to pick up on their different artistic interests, and he couldn't help but smile at how diverse their talents were.

The girl with the easel said she loved painting landscapes inspired by nature, while the guitar player mentioned a passion for songwriting. With each introduction, Kyle felt the atmosphere shift to one of camaraderie and shared enthusiasm, and he knew this class would be a unique experience. It was finally Kyle's turn to introduce himself, and as he stood up, he felt a mix of excitement and nerves coursing through him. "Hi, I'm Kyle," he said, his voice steady despite the flutter of butterflies in his stomach. "I love to draw, read books, and write poetry. I also enjoy collecting quotes that inspire me." He felt a bit sheepish sharing that, aware that many others had unique talents, but it was his truth.

As the introductions wrapped up, Mrs. Arya turned her attention to the board and noticed the quote Kyle had written earlier. A look of surprise crossed her face. "Who wrote this?" she asked, her eyebrows raised in curiosity.
Kyle instinctively raised his hand. "That would be me," he replied, a bit sheepishly.

"Is it an original quote?" she inquired; her interest piqued. Kyle shook his head. "Not quite. I wish I could say it was, but I lack the experience to come up with something profound, at least not yet. I usually pick up quotes from books or listen to what great philosophers have to say." Mrs. Arya smiled warmly at him. "Well, I appreciate your honesty, Kyle. It takes a lot to share your thoughts and experiences. Keep seeking inspiration, and you'll find your voice in no time." Her encouragement made him feel a little more at ease, and he returned her smile with genuine appreciation.
After a moment, she clapped her hands together, drawing everyone's attention once more. "Now, I'd like each of you to present your talents to the class. This will help us get to know each other better and foster a supportive environment. You'll have one hour to prepare!"

A buzz of excitement filled the room as students began to discuss what they would showcase. Some pulled out sketchbooks, while others strummed their guitars or flipped through notebooks for lyrics. Kyle could feel the energy shift as everyone dove into their preparations, each one of them ready to share a piece of themselves with the class. The atmosphere was charged with creativity, and he couldn't help but feel thrilled to be part of it. As the time ticked away, Kyle felt a wave of anxiety wash over him. The reality of the presentation set in, and he began to worry. What could he showcase that would impress the class? Drawing was the only thing he felt comfortable with, and while he understood people's emotions deeply, there was no way to present that directly. His mind raced with thoughts of all the great poets and philosophers he admired, but he knew he hadn't yet formed their wisdom into anything tangible.

With no other choice, he decided to pour his feelings into his art. He grabbed his sketchpad and pencils, determined to make something meaningful. Looking around, he observed his classmates as they busily prepared. Some were painting vibrant canvases, while others practiced songs, their voices harmonizing beautifully. A few students strummed guitars, filling the room with melodies that lifted the atmosphere. The excitement of creativity surrounded him, but Kyle felt a pang of self-doubt.

Focusing on his drawing, he envisioned his bike parked under the glowing evening sunset. He could almost hear the soft patter of rain as he sketched, capturing the moment when the last rays of sunlight reflected off the dew drops that clung to his bike. He meticulously added details—the sleek curves of the frame, the glint of the handlebars, and the vibrant colors of the sunset blending with the clouds. Each stroke of his pencil brought the image to life, and as he worked, he found himself lost in the rhythm of creation. When he finally stepped back to examine his sketch, a wave of satisfaction washed over him. The image resonated with the beauty of nature and the essence of a peaceful moment—his bike, a symbol of freedom and adventure, surrounded by the warmth of the setting sun. He felt a sense of accomplishment, knowing that this piece represented not just his love for art but also a slice of his world. Kyle took a deep breath, ready to share this part of himself with his classmates, feeling more confident than before.

As the clock ticked closer to the end of the preparation hour, the energy in the classroom shifted from nervous excitement to a buzz of creativity. One by one, students began to present their work, showcasing their unique talents. Kate was the first up, her hands trembling slightly as she unveiled a stunning drawing of her cat. The level of detail was impressive; you could see the playful gleam in the cat's eyes and the soft texture of its fur. The class erupted in applause, and

Kyle couldn't help but smile at how effortlessly she had captured her pet's personality.

Next was Sean, who confidently plugged his keyboard into the outlet. As his fingers danced across the keys, a melody filled the room that had everyone tapping their feet. He skillfully played an upbeat tune, demonstrating not only his talent but also his passion for music. Kyle found himself clapping along, impressed by the camaraderie forming within the classroom.

The presentations continued, each student revealing something special: a poem recited with heartfelt emotion, a painting that captured a breathtaking landscape, and a passionate performance on a guitar. Kyle watched in awe as each person shared their creativity, feeling inspired by the diverse expressions of art around him. When it was finally his turn, Kyle stood up with a mixture of excitement and nerves. He stepped forward, holding his sketch proudly. "This is my bike," he began, a smile breaking across his face. "I have a real passion for riding. It's not just about the freedom; it's about the places it takes me and the moments I get to experience along the way." As he explained the details of his drawing—the dew drops glistening in the sunlight, the warmth of the sunset—he felt a sense of connection with his classmates, sharing not just a piece of art, but a piece of himself.

When everyone finished their presentations, Mrs. Arya stood before the class with a beaming smile. "I have to say, this is the best class I have had in my career," she announced, her enthusiasm infectious. Applause erupted, and the atmosphere was filled with a collective sense of accomplishment and joy. "Now, I should mention," she continued, "one of our students has dropped out, leaving us with 19 in total. However, we will be welcoming a new student, Autumn, starting next class."

"Autumn, huh?" Kyle mused to himself, intrigued by the name as he packed up his sketchpad and supplies. It was a unique name that seemed to promise a unique personality. With a sense of anticipation, he headed out of the classroom, eager to meet his friends at football practice, ready to share his day and hear about theirs. Kyle settled down on the wooden bench in the locker room, his football bag resting beside him. As he began unpacking, he could hear his friends' laughter echoing down the hallway. The door swung open, and in walked Sam, Nate, and Ryder, each wearing wide smiles that conveyed their excitement.

"Guys, you won't believe the class I just had!" Sam exclaimed, his voice booming with energy. "I mean, it's just management studies, but my professor is a former startup CEO! He's already dropping wisdom like it's a competition. I can't wait to learn from him. He even shared his first investment blunder with us. It was a total disaster but hilarious in hindsight. Let's just say a vending machine full of kale chips didn't exactly take off!"

Nate rolled his eyes playfully. "I'm just glad I'm not the only one who got an interesting class. We had a guest speaker in business studies—a successful entrepreneur who turned his hobby into a multi-million dollar company. He started as a kid selling handmade bracelets, and now he's all about sustainability in fashion. He really inspired us to think outside the box. I mean, if a kid selling bracelets can do it, what's stopping us?"

"Probably a lack of bracelet-making skills," Ryder chimed in with a smirk. "But seriously, that's awesome, Nate. I'm more interested in the networking opportunities, though. I met a guy who's already working on some app for managing finances. He said he'd show me the ropes if I wanted to get into that. And of course, I told him I'd happily join in. You know me, always on the lookout for the next big thing."

Kyle chuckled, feeling a surge of camaraderie as he listened to his friends share their stories. "I think all your classes sound way more interesting than art. I just drew a picture of my bike today," he said, trying to keep a humble tone.

"Oh, come on! A bike? You could have done better

than that," Sam teased, nudging Kyle with his elbow. "But seriously, your drawings are great, man. You need to show us some of your other work sometime."

"Definitely! You know how I love to blend emotions into my art," Kyle replied, a little shyly. "But honestly, it's been a lot of pressure. Everyone's so talented, and I just... I don't know if I can measure up."

"Don't sweat it," Nate said, his tone reassuring. "Everyone has their own style. You're not just a guy who draws; you've got a unique perspective that nobody else has. Just keep doing you." With their banter flowing and the locker room filling with the scent of sweat and grass, Kyle felt lighter. Each of his friends was bringing their unique strengths and stories into their academic journeys, reminding him that they were all in this together.

As they settled in, lacing up their cleats and grabbing their gear, Kyle looked around at the familiar faces of his friends. He realized that despite their different paths, they were all searching for their own versions of success, cheering each other on every step of the way. "Alright, enough chit-chat," Ryder said, standing up and throwing his bag over his shoulder. "Let's hit the field and show them how it's done!"

Just as they were about to leave the locker room, Sam paused and looked around. "Wait a minute, where's Ryan? I thought he was right behind us."

Before anyone could respond, Ryan burst through the door, looking absolutely bewildered. His hair was slightly disheveled, and his expression shifted between confusion and mild embarrassment. "Guys, you won't believe what just happened," he said, shaking his head in disbelief. "What's up?" Nate asked, raising an eyebrow, a teasing smile creeping onto his face.

"I asked a girl out," Ryan admitted, his voice barely above a whisper, "and she said no. That was my first time being rejected, and I'm trying to figure out what I did wrong!" The others erupted into playful teasing. Sam chuckled, shaking his head. "Wow, Ryan, it's the first day of classes, and you're already asking someone out? At this rate, you're going to run out of options before the week's even over!"

"Yeah," Ryder added, grinning. "You might want to work on your pitch, though. Did you mention your computer science skills? That's a surefire way to win hearts!" Kyle laughed along with the banter but then asked, "So, how did your class go, aside from the whole 'rejection' drama?" Ryan shrugged, still looking somewhat pensive. "It was alright. The professor's pretty experienced for his age. He even shared some real-world stories about coding and tech that were actually interesting."

After a bit more ribbing and laughter, Ryan quickly changed into his football attire, and the group headed out to the field, the teasing fading into excitement.

As they approached, they noticed several new faces among the players. The new students began whispering amongst themselves, glancing at Kyle and his friends. Kyle exchanged amused glances with the group. "Looks like our reputation precedes us," he said with a smirk, striding confidently towards the center of the field where their team was gathering. Once they reached their teammates, Sam looked around and asked, "So, anyone new here who's going to pose a challenge to us this year?"

Just as he finished speaking, a loud crack echoed across the field, and everyone turned to see a soccer ball soaring toward the goal. A tall guy, clearly a new transfer, had just executed an impressive kick. He jogged over to Kyle and the group, a confident grin plastered on his face. "Hey! I'm Alex, the new guy," he said, extending his hand. "Heard you all are the team to beat this year."

Kyle shook his hand firmly, a spark of excitement igniting in his chest. "Looks like we've got competition this year!" he replied, feeling the thrill of rivalry brewing between their team and the newcomers. The air buzzed with potential challenges as they prepared to hit the field. After igniting a rivalry with the new transfers, everyone practiced extra hard, pushing themselves to the limit on the field. The drills had been intense, but as the sun dipped lower in the sky, exhaustion began to settle in. When the practice finally wrapped up, they packed their gear, their bodies aching but spirits high, and set off for home. As they rode their bikes down the hill in silence, the late afternoon breeze brushed against their faces, a welcome reprieve after the practice. Each of them was lost in their thoughts, reflecting on the day's excitement and the fierce competition that lay ahead.

When Kyle finally reached home, he was greeted by the enticing aroma of his mom's cooking wafting through the air. "Dinner smells amazing!" he called out as he stepped inside, dropping his backpack by the door.

His mom poked her head out of the kitchen, a bright smile on her face. "Thanks! I made your favorite—spaghetti and garlic bread. How was your day?"

Kyle settled at the table, the warmth of the meal bringing a sense of comfort. "It was great! We started new classes today, and I finally got to introduce myself in art. I even wrote a quote on the board, and everyone loved it!" He paused, eyes sparkling with excitement. "And then we had football practice. There are some new transfers, and they're pretty good. We have real competition this year!" His mom listened intently, her eyes lighting up with each detail. "Wow, that sounds amazing, Kyle! I'm so glad you're enjoying your classes. I can't wait to hear more about your art projects and football games."

After dinner, Kyle helped clear the table, feeling a sense of satisfaction from the day. He retreated to his room, the day's events replaying in his mind like a movie. The exhaustion washed over him as he changed into his pajamas, and within moments of lying down, he drifted off to sleep, dreaming of colorful canvases, football fields, and the adventures yet to come.

The next day began like any other, the sun rising to reveal a world of possibilities. It was now the second day of art class, and Kyle, as usual, arrived early. He settled into his seat and let out a contented sigh, relishing the peaceful atmosphere. However, his eyes were soon drawn to an empty bag resting a few seats in front of him. He remembered Mrs. Arya mentioning that a student would be joining the class today, sparking a flicker of curiosity in him. With the classroom still deserted, he decided to take a stroll around the corridor.

As he wandered through the hallway, Kyle peered into Sam's classroom, which was just down the way. He spotted Sam animatedly chatting with some classmates, his usual charismatic self. A smirk spread across Kyle's face as he waved at Sam, who noticed him and waved back enthusiastically. Feeling a little mischievous, Kyle strolled into Sam's classroom and plopped down at his desk.

"Hey, my class hasn't started yet, so I thought I'd drop by. Feeling a bit bored, you know?" Kyle said, leaning back in his chair, his fingers drumming lightly on the desk. "Bored? On the second day? You're already slacking!" Sam teased; a grin plastered across his face. "Let me introduce you to everyone. Guys, this is Kyle. He's our resident artist and philosopher."

Kyle chuckled as Sam introduced him to a few classmates nearby. They greeted him with friendly smiles and nods, clearly amused by Sam's playful antics. The lively chatter filled the room as Sam continued to draw Kyle into the conversation.
Just then, Sam's professor entered the room, a tall figure with an approachable demeanor and a knowing smile. Kyle quickly stood up, realizing he had overstayed his welcome. "Sorry, I didn't mean to intrude!" he said.

The professor waved him off with a chuckle. "No problem at all! You're welcome to join if you want to learn anything. Just make sure to take good notes!"

With a grin, Kyle took that as his cue to make a quick exit. He stepped back into the hallway, his mind buzzing from the brief visit with Sam. As he made his way to his own classroom, he noticed Mrs. Arya just walking in, her presence filling the corridor with a sense of anticipation. Quickening his pace, he hurried behind her, keeping his head down to avoid drawing attention. As he walked past his classmates, he focused on his desk, determined to settle in before class began. Taking a deep breath, he prepared himself for another day filled with creativity and new experiences. As everyone settled into their seats, a gentle hum of excitement filled the air, sparking the beginning of another creative day. Mrs. Arya stood at the front, her warm, enthusiastic smile instantly grabbing their attention. "Alright, class," she began, clapping her hands to draw them in. "The cultural festival is approaching, and this year, it's up to all of you to come up with a unique presentation to showcase your talents."

A wave of murmurs and eager discussions spread across the room as students leaned toward each other, bouncing ideas around. Some were whispering about live music performances, others about putting together an art exhibition, and a few even suggested poetry recitals. Kyle glanced around, noticing the familiar faces he'd only briefly interacted with before. He didn't know any of them too well but realized he'd have to join in and share his thoughts if he wanted to contribute.

Reluctantly, he shifted his seat toward a nearby group of classmates. They welcomed him into their conversation, and soon, ideas were flowing. "How about a performance that combines art and music?" one girl suggested, her eyes bright with excitement. "We could paint or sketch while someone plays an instrument!"

Another student chimed in, "Or maybe something that includes live poetry, with background music. It would feel artistic and different." Kyle nodded, impressed by their enthusiasm. He found himself throwing out suggestions too, his ideas meeting with nods and murmurs of approval. Before long, they settled on a plan: a mixed presentation involving live sketching, accompanied by music and spoken word. It felt ambitious, but the challenge of blending their talents made everyone's eyes light up.

When they shared their idea with Mrs. Arya, she smiled and nodded, clearly pleased with their decision. "Wonderful! That sounds unique. I can't wait to see what you all create," she encouraged, clapping her hands as a signal that class was wrapping up.

As they gathered their things, Kyle's thoughts drifted. He realized he'd been so caught up in the group discussions that he hadn't noticed Autumn all class. She was in her seat, quietly putting her supplies away, her face still somewhat of a mystery. Though she'd been introduced briefly yesterday, she hadn't shared much about herself, and he hadn't seen her work yet. Kyle found his attention lingering on her for a moment. She seemed different somehow, and he couldn't quite place why. "Who is she, really?" he wondered, feeling a strange curiosity bloom inside him.

The following evening, after a long day, Kyle's usual routine fell into place. Exhausted, he went to bed, drifting off with the quiet, familiar comfort that came at the end of each day. For Kyle, being somewhat introverted meant he rarely initiated conversations with strangers—he tended to keep to himself unless someone approached him first. That was just how he was.

The next day, as he walked toward the art class, he spotted Autumn ahead, trying to adjust her desk, which was facing the window. She looked like she was struggling a little, and without a second thought, Kyle decided to lend a hand. He approached her silently, clearing his throat softly to catch her attention. Autumn looked up, a bit startled, but then stepped back as Kyle moved in to shift the desk.

Kyle adjusted Autumn's desk with a quick, gentle shove, stepping back and nodding to himself as the desk settled into place. She turned toward him, and for a moment, the afternoon sunlight streaming through the window caught her face, casting a soft glow that made him pause. Her eyes met his, and he was momentarily struck by their unusual color—a deep, warm blend of orange and brown that seemed to reflect the golden light in the room.

It was almost as if her eyes were capturing the very essence of her name, carrying the warmth and richness of autumn leaves. They held a depth, like a quiet forest in fall, full of subtle shifts and hidden colors. Kyle realized with a start that he was staring, and as she brushed a strand of hair behind her ear, she broke the silence.

"Thank you," she said softly, her voice gentle, almost musical. The simple words were polite and kind, yet something about the way she said them made them feel genuine.

Kyle swallowed, managing a small, warm smile, but as he returned to his seat, his mind felt strangely foggy. He sat down, still feeling the impact of that brief exchange. Thoughts came and went, scattered and disconnected, as if his mind had slipped out of focus. For a moment, he couldn't even remember what he had planned to do next. All he could recall was the softness of her voice, the way her eyes had glowed with that autumn warmth.

Settling into his chair, he shook his head slightly, trying to clear his mind. But even as he focused on the class around him, the image of her eyes lingered, like the lingering scent of something warm and familiar. It left him feeling both calm and oddly unsettled, as if he'd stumbled upon a quiet mystery that would stay with him, just out of reach.

Kyle couldn't shake the strange feeling lingering in his chest—a subtle, inexplicable pull toward Autumn. It was like a whisper at the back of his mind, hinting that something significant was unfolding, even if he couldn't quite grasp what. Try as he might to focus on the teacher's words, his attention kept drifting forward to where Autumn sat, just a couple of seats away. He found himself glancing at her every few moments, catching glimpses of her thick black hair glistening in the golden afternoon sunlight, cascading over her shoulders. There was a quiet confidence about her, a calmness that only deepened his curiosity.

Time seemed to slip by faster than usual, and before he knew it, the class was over. His classmates began gathering their things, chatting as they shuffled toward the door. Kyle, however, felt glued to his seat, as if leaving would break the delicate thread tying him to whatever mystery he felt around her. He lingered as the room emptied, his eyes absentmindedly drifting to the window, lost in thought.

He sighed, the quiet classroom amplifying the sound. He didn't know why, but he felt as if he needed just one more look into those eyes, as if it would anchor him, help him understand this strange sensation. His thoughts wandered deeper, and before he knew it, nearly twenty minutes had passed, leaving him alone in the stillness of the room.

Suddenly, a sharp nudge jolted him back to reality. He turned, startled, to see Sam standing behind him, grinning. "Well, look who's in la-la land," Sam teased, crossing his arms. "Didn't realize the view from here was that mesmerizing."

Kyle felt his face flush as he stumbled to respond. "I was just... thinking. Lost in thought."

"Yeah, right," Sam chuckled, clearly amused. "Thoughts about a certain someone, maybe?" His smirk grew, knowing he'd hit the mark. "It's written all over your face, Picasso."
Kyle rubbed the back of his neck, a shy smile breaking through. He didn't deny it, but he didn't confirm anything either, leaving Sam with a satisfied chuckle as they made their way out together.

They made their way to the field, where the rest of their friends were already warming up for practice. The atmosphere was filled with energy and a sense of friendly rivalry after their recent challenge from the new transfers.

As practice got underway, Kyle tried to focus, but every now and then, his gaze wandered up to the top-floor window of the art classroom. The thought of

Autumn lingered in his mind, and he couldn't resist the occasional glance in that direction.

In the middle of a drill, Nate caught him looking and raised an eyebrow. "You keep looking up there. What's got your attention?"

Kyle shrugged, brushing it off with a quick grin. "Just... thought I saw something, that's all."

Nate chuckled, clearly not buying it, but he let it slide. They wrapped up their practice after some intense drills, each of them sweaty and exhausted. As the sun began to set, they packed up and headed home, splitting off in their usual directions.

When Kyle got home, his mom immediately noticed the glow on his face. "Something different about today?" she asked, her eyes sparkling with curiosity.

"Why do you ask?" Kyle replied, trying to play it cool.

She gave him a knowing look. "You've got this... glow about you. Like you're lit up from the inside."

Kyle chuckled, running a hand through his hair. "Maybe it was just a good practice match. We were pretty pumped up today."

He went up to his room afterward, but his thoughts

kept circling back to the day, especially to those moments he'd caught himself thinking about Autumn. With a sigh, he lay down, realizing it might not be so easy to shake her from his mind. The Next day set in as the sun peeked through the clouds, casting a warm glow over the campus, Kyle arrived at class, feeling a mix of anticipation and nervousness. As he walked in, he immediately noticed Autumn struggling with the window, tugging at the handle with a frown on her face.

A smile crept onto Kyle's lips at the sight—he could relate to her frustration. Without thinking twice, he made his way over, offering a hand. "Need some help?" he asked, the words tumbling out before he could second-guess himself.
She looked up at him, her expression lighting up as she nodded. "That would be great!" With a firm tug, Kyle managed to free the stubborn window, and it swung open with a satisfying creak. The fresh air rushed in, and Autumn turned to him, her eyes sparkling. "Thank you so much!"

But this time, Kyle felt an overwhelming urge to avoid her gaze. He feared that if he looked into those captivating eyes, he would lose himself all over again. "No problem," he replied, keeping his tone casual as he turned back to his seat.

Once settled, he tried to push thoughts of her aside, focusing instead on his work. But it was no use;

the feeling in his chest was like a persistent whisper, reminding him of how much he wanted to understand this strange attraction. He wished he could just forget her and quell the unease that seemed to have taken root inside him. As more students filtered into the classroom, Kyle observed Autumn engaging with everyone around her. Her laughter echoed like music, and she had a natural way of making everyone feel included. It was clear she was the opposite of him—outgoing, animated, and effortlessly drawing people in with her joyful aura. She exuded a warmth that made it seem like happiness followed her wherever she went. Kyle kept his head down, diligently working on his assignments, trying to block out the laughter and chatter around him. Despite his efforts, he couldn't shake the sense that being near Autumn was like standing in the sun; it brought light but also made him feel a little exposed, a little vulnerable. He couldn't quite comprehend how one person could make him feel both curious and uneasy at the same time. It had been two days since Autumn had joined the art class, and during that time, Kyle had remained silent, caught in a whirlwind of thoughts and feelings he couldn't quite understand. But today was different. As he entered the classroom, a mix of anticipation and anxiety bubbled within him. While he was making his way to his usual seat, he heard her voice call out, "Hey." The sound was bright and inviting, cutting through the haze of his thoughts. Turning towards her, Kyle felt his heart race when she asked, "How was your day?"

In that moment, her question felt like the most important thing in the world. Kyle stood beside her desk, his heart pounding in his chest. "It was good," he said, trying to keep his voice steady. "Football practice was intense today. We're working hard since we have a new rivalry with some transfer students." He felt the words flow out of him, detailing how he hung out with his friends afterward, how they joked and laughed, all while staring out the window, the familiar scenery blurring past as he avoided making direct eye contact with her.

As he spoke, he could feel the warmth radiating from her, her presence somehow calming yet exhilarating. He wanted to take in every detail of her expression, but he was terrified of what he might find in her eyes. Just as he was gathering the courage to glance at her, the door swung open, and Mrs. Arya stepped into the classroom, her enthusiasm filling the air.

"Alright, everyone! Let's settle down!" she called, her eyes sparkling with energy. Autumn, in a move that took Kyle by surprise, gestured for him to sit at the desk right next to her—the seat that had been empty since the class began. "Come sit here!" she said, a bright smile on her face.

Kyle's heart raced again, but this time with nervous excitement. He slid into the chair beside her, feeling a rush of warmth wash over him. It was a new experience, sitting so close to her, and he couldn't shake the feeling that this moment marked a shift in their dynamic. With his palms slightly sweaty and his mind racing, he wondered how this would go. Would he be able to speak to her without getting tongue-tied? Would they find common ground amidst the chaos of their differences? All he could do was hope for the best as he settled into his seat, his pulse quickening with the uncertainty of what lay ahead. As the class began, a familiar hum of creativity filled the air. Students settled into their tasks, paintbrushes danced across canvases, and the sound of pencil on paper resonated throughout the room.

"You seem very silent," Autumn remarked, breaking the comfortable silence between them. She turned to him with a curious smile, her warm gaze encouraging him to share more.

"I'm just a bit of an introvert," Kyle replied softly, the words slipping out more easily than he had anticipated.

Autumn considered his words for a moment, her expression thoughtful. "Actually," she said, "I would want to be like you, minding my own business without worrying about what everyone thinks. It seems peaceful." Kyle was taken aback by her response. "Really? You'd rather be quiet and reserved?" he asked, intrigued. The idea that she would envy his introversion felt foreign, yet it sparked something within him.

"Yeah," she replied, a hint of sincerity in her voice. "Sometimes it feels like a lot of pressure to always be 'on.' It must be nice to just observe without all that noise." Kyle nodded, reflecting on her words. "I get that. But I want to be more like you, too—getting to know a lot of people and just speaking to almost everyone. You make it seem easy."

Autumn smiled, and for a moment, they were both caught in the shared understanding of their differences. As the conversation flowed, they began to delve deeper into their lives, their interests, and their experiences. Autumn's laughter was infectious, and Kyle felt himself relax in her presence. It was a refreshing change, and for the first time in a long while, he found himself opening up, comfortable being himself without the pressure of needing to impress.

As the minutes ticked by, the world outside the classroom faded, leaving just the two of them in their own bubble of conversation. It was a small yet significant step toward breaking down the barriers that had kept him silent for so long. Kyle couldn't help but feel grateful for the connection they were forming, each shared thought and laughter drawing them closer.

Just then, the bell rang, signaling the end of class. Kyle gathered his belongings, He turned to Autumn, who was still organizing her art supplies. "I've got football practice now, but I'll catch up with you tomorrow," he said, trying to sound casual despite the fluttering in his stomach.

"Okay! Take care," she replied, her voice warm and genuine.

As those words lingered in the air, Kyle felt his heart start to race. That simple farewell sent a rush of adrenaline through him, and for a moment, his mind went blank. He couldn't remember the last time a girl had spoken to him with such kindness. It was a small gesture, but it resonated deeply, making him feel seen in a way he hadn't experienced before.

With a goofy grin plastered on his face, he hurried out of the classroom, practically buzzing with excitement. He couldn't wait to find Sam and share what had happened. The hallway felt more vibrant as he walked, every corner filled with a sense of possibility.

At the practice field, he quickly located his friends. They were gathered near the benches, laughing and joking as they prepared for the session. Kyle called Sam aside, trying to keep his enthusiasm in check. "Hey, can we talk after practice? I need to tell you something."

"Sure, man. What's up?" Sam replied, raising an eyebrow with curiosity.

As practice concluded, Kyle nudged Ryan, Ryder, and Nate. "You guys go ahead. Sam and I need to pick something up," he said, dismissing them with a wave. They nodded, exchanging playful smirks, clearly curious about what was brewing between the two. Once they were alone, Kyle turned to Sam, his heart pounding with anticipation. "It's about this girl Autumn," he started, his voice barely containing his excitement. "She's amazing! You should've seen her in class—she has this way of talking to everyone, and she's just... so confident."

Sam crossed his arms, a knowing smile creeping onto his face. "Go on," he urged, enjoying the rare sight of Kyle so animated. Kyle continued, practically bouncing on his feet. "When I opened the window for her, she actually thanked me! I mean, it's just a simple thing, but the way she said it felt... different. I don't know how to explain it."

Sam laughed, shaking his head. "I wanna see where this goes, man. You're totally smitten. Just don't mess it up, alright?"

Kyle chuckled, the reality of his feelings dawning on him. "I know, I know! I just... I want to get to know her better. I'll keep you updated." The prospect of tomorrow filled him with anticipation—this was just the beginning of something new, and Kyle was ready to embrace it.

Just like that, the week slipped away, each day dragging a little longer than the last for Kyle. It was as if time itself had slowed, and every tick of the clock served as a reminder of how much he missed speaking with Autumn. He found it hard to concentrate in class, his thoughts constantly drifting back to her laughter, her smile, and the warmth of their brief conversations. It felt as if a part of him had been left with her, and he couldn't quite figure out how to retrieve it.

His emotions were a chaotic swirl, a blend of excitement and nervousness that he couldn't put into words. The feeling was new and overwhelming, and Kyle had never been good at navigating the complexities of crushes. He just knew that he needed to see her again, to feel that connection spark between them once more. As the weekend approached, he and his friends decided to gather at their usual spot—the serene hilltop overlooking their small town. It had become a sanctuary for them, a place where they could escape the pressures of school and simply enjoy each other's company. They spent hours there, sharing stories, laughing, and teasing one another, but the underlying tension of Kyle's unspoken feelings lingered in the back of his mind.

When Monday finally arrived, The familiar rhythm of school would soon return, and with it, the hope of seeing Autumn again. As he entered the school building, he could already feel his heart racing. Would she say hello? Would he muster the courage to approach her?

His thoughts were a chaotic jumble as he navigated the hallways, but he was determined to make the most of the day. He could hardly wait for art class, counting down the minutes until he could see her and perhaps bridge the gap that had formed between them over the last few days. Monday held a promise, and Kyle was ready to embrace whatever came next.

As the art class began, Kyle made his way to his desk beside Autumn, his heart fluttering with anticipation. This was the moment he had been waiting for since their last conversation. With a friendly smile, he asked, "How was your weekend?"

Autumn chuckled, a light and melodic sound that made Kyle's heart race. "Oh, you know, I just like to laze around and do nothing all day—just sleep!"

Kyle grinned, leaning back in his chair. "That sounds like a very good way to spend a weekend. Sometimes I think we all need a little downtime." She nodded, her eyes sparkling with mischief. "Yeah, but I also sing sometimes. Just when I'm alone, though. I don't think anyone would want to hear me!"

The way she said it, with a hint of shyness mixed with pride, captivated Kyle. He couldn't help but wonder how her voice would sound, echoing through the empty hallways, or perhaps harmonizing with the chirping birds outside. "I bet you have a beautiful voice," he whispered to himself, not realizing how he had said it aloud until Autumn turned to him, a curious smile on her lips.

They soon fell into a comfortable rhythm of conversation, sharing snippets of their high school stories. Kyle found himself animatedly recounting adventures with his friends—the wild rides on their bikes, the impromptu road trips to nearby towns, and the silly pranks they pulled on each other. As he spoke, he watched Autumn's expressions shift from amusement to genuine interest, and it filled him with a sense of joy he hadn't experienced in a long time.

In the midst of their chat, he remembered the drawings he had done on the first day of art class. With a sudden burst of excitement, he pulled out his sketchbook and flipped to the page where his bike sketch was. "Check this out," he said, showing her the detailed image.

Autumn leaned in closer, her gaze intense and appreciative as she examined his work. "Wow, this is really impressive!" she exclaimed, her voice filled with admiration. "You have a real talent, Kyle. Can you draw a portrait? I would love to see what you could do!" The request took Kyle by surprise, but the thought of capturing her likeness on paper thrilled him. "I could definitely try," he replied, feeling a wave of inspiration wash over him. The idea of spending more time with her, pouring his creativity into a portrait, felt like an exciting opportunity—a way to blend his passion with a growing connection.

As they continued their conversation, Autumn leaned in with a playful curiosity. "So, who would you draw a portrait of?" she asked, a teasing glint in her eye that made Kyle's heart race

Kyle already knew the answer, but he decided to stall for a moment, pretending to scan the classroom for someone beautiful to draw. "Hmm, I'm not sure. I need to find someone truly stunning," he replied, his voice light and playful, a smile tugging at the corners of his mouth. Autumn laughed, her eyes sparkling with mischief. "More than me?" she challenged, leaning back in her seat with mock disbelief.

Kyle smirked, decided to play along. "Your beauty cannot be captured on a canvas," he said, his tone light yet sincere. Her cheeks flushed a soft pink as she laughed it off, brushing away the compliment with a casual wave of her hand. "I knew you'd say something like that!" she replied, giggling, but there was a hint of shyness in her voice that made Kyle's heart skip a beat.

In that moment, he felt a rush of admiration for her. It wasn't just her looks that captivated him; it was the way she carried herself, the infectious joy she exuded, and the effortless way she connected with those around her. He glanced at her, realizing that what he had said was more than just a flirty comment; it was the truth he had only begun to understand. The realization settled in his chest like a soft glow.

As their laughter faded, Kyle found himself momentarily lost in thought, imagining what it would be like to draw her—capturing her essence on paper while hearing her sing. The idea filled him with anticipation and a tinge of anxiety, and he silently hoped that this playful exchange would lead to something deeper between them.

"Maybe we could make it a challenge," Kyle suggested, his voice growing a little bolder. "If I draw a portrait of you, you should sing a song for me."

Autumn's eyes widened in surprise, her enthusiasm shining through. "Deal! But you have to promise it won't be some kind of abstract interpretation of me," she joked, her laughter ringing like music in the air.

"I promise," Kyle replied, grinning. "Just let me know when you're ready to pose."

As they shared this moment, Kyle felt a sense of connection blossoming between them, one that felt electric and full of possibility. He knew that what started as a simple conversation had opened the door to something much more significant, and he couldn't wait to see where it would lead.

As the week drew to a close, Kyle found himself reflecting on the blossoming friendship he had with Autumn. Every day seemed to weave them closer together, their contrasting personalities creating a unique harmony that intrigued him. He often caught himself gazing at her during class, fascinated by the way her laughter could light up the room. Autumn had etched her image in his mind, each detail vivid: the playful bounce of her thick black hair, the warmth of her orange-brown eyes, and the way her smile felt like sunshine.

On a sunny Friday afternoon, as they packed up after art class, Autumn approached Kyle with an invitation that made his heart skip a beat. "Hey, how about I pose for you this weekend?" she suggested, her enthusiasm infectious. Kyle smiled, excitement bubbling beneath the surface. "You don't need to worry about that right now. Just focus on practicing your song for Monday," he replied, keeping the anticipation alive. They both laughed, sharing a moment of connection as they parted ways, eager for what was to come. Later that afternoon, Kyle met up with his friends at the football practice field. The air was charged with energy as they stretched and prepared for their session. After a vigorous warm-up, Ryan piped up with a grin, "My brother has a football match this weekend. You guys want to come?"

The group exchanged eager looks, but Kyle felt a slight tightening in his chest. "I can't make it," he said, trying to sound casual. "I have something important to attend to."

Ryan raised an eyebrow, sensing there was more to it. "Important, huh?" he teased, but Kyle just smiled, keeping his thoughts about Autumn to himself. Sam, standing nearby, caught the glint in Kyle's eye, clearly in on the secret.

As they finished practice and began to make plans for the weekend, Kyle's mind lingered on Autumn. The weekend stretched before him, full of hope. As soon as Kyle arrived home, the familiar warmth of his mother's greeting enveloped him. "Hey, sweetheart! How was your day?" she asked, setting aside a pot on the stove and giving him a warm smile.

"It was good, Mom," Kyle replied, his mind already buzzing with thoughts of Autumn. After dinner, filled with the comforting flavors of home, he retreated to his room, eager to process the day.

Sinking into his chair, he began talking to himself, a habit he had developed when deep in thought. “She must be wondering how I’ll draw her without her being present,” he mused aloud, a small smile creeping onto his face. The thought of Autumn posing for him sparked his imagination, and he felt a rush of excitement at the prospect.

He stared at the blank sketchbook resting on his desk, determined to start drawing tomorrow. “I’ll make it special,” he promised himself, envisioning the lines and shadows he would create to capture her essence.

With that thought in mind, Kyle slipped under his covers, satisfied with how everything was starting to pan out. His heart swelled with hope, and as he closed his eyes, he drifted off to sleep, dreaming of vibrant colors, laughter, and the enchanting voice of the girl who had somehow turned his world upside down.

Kyle awoke early, a rush of excitement coursing through him as the sunlight streamed through his window. Today felt different, infused with warmth. After freshening up, he headed to the kitchen where the warm aroma of breakfast greeted him. His mom looked up from the kitchen, smiling.

“I’ll be busy today,” he said, a hint of anticipation in his voice.

"Busy with what? Another art project?" she teased, knowing well the joy he found in his sketches.

"Something like that," he replied, gathering his art supplies. Once outside, he felt the fresh air fill his lungs as he walked to his room. He took a moment to close his eyes, letting his mind drift to thoughts of Autumn. He envisioned her in the perfect pose, one that would capture her essence. The image formed in his mind—a vision of her sitting by the window, her hair tousled by a gentle breeze. This wasn't just any scene to him; it was the moment he'd felt a strange, unspoken connection. He could still feel the rush of his heart that day, the subtle thrill of standing so close to her. He knew he had to do justice to this memory, as if by preserving it on paper, he could hold onto that feeling just a little longer.

In that moment, Kyle could see the sunlight filtering through the glass, illuminating each strand of her hair like golden threads. He imagined the light dancing across her face, enhancing the warmth of her skin and making her eyes shimmer with depth, the orange hues blending seamlessly with the light. It was an ethereal vision, as if she had stepped out of a fantasy world, and he was determined to capture it.

With renewed purpose, he set to work on the canvas, letting his pencil glide across the paper as he poured every ounce of admiration and detail into his drawing. The hours slipped by as he lost himself in the art, each stroke a tribute to her beauty. When he finally leaned back to admire his work, a sigh of relief escaped his lips. "I tried my best to recreate you," he murmured, but a twinge of dissatisfaction gnawed at him. It wasn't that the artwork wasn't good—he knew it was exceptional. But it felt like a mere shadow of her true beauty, a fleeting glimpse rather than the full spectrum of what made Autumn who she was. He packed away his supplies, a sense of longing in his chest as he prepared for the next day. Tonight, he would let the excitement of what tomorrow might bring lull him to sleep, dreaming of the moment he would finally share his creation with her.

Monday arrived, and Kyle could feel the subtle thrill of anticipation as he carefully placed the finished sketch in his bag, making sure it lay flat and secure. He barely noticed breakfast, his mind focused on the upcoming art class and Autumn's reaction when she finally saw the portrait. After a quick goodbye to his mom, he was off, riding to the university with a new energy, the morning sun reflecting his own excitement.

The day went by in a blur of lectures and conversations, each hour building his anticipation. Finally, after lunch, it was time. As he made his way to the art room, he caught sight of Autumn standing near the door, a curious glint in her eyes that made him smile. She looked as though she'd been waiting, her gaze shifting to him as he approached, her expression a mix of excitement and mystery. They didn't need to say anything—their shared looks said enough.

Kyle walked into the classroom and took his seat, his heart racing as he settled in, the portrait safely hidden in his bag. Autumn took her own seat nearby, and for the next hour, their interactions were wordless but electric. She'd glance over at him with a small, knowing smile, and he'd respond with a grin, feeling his pulse quicken every time their eyes met. The two of them seemed to be sharing a secret that only they understood, their silent exchanges filled with playful suspense. As the teacher continued, Autumn and Kyle remained absorbed in their own little world, barely able to contain their excitement. Kyle could feel the anticipation building with each passing minute, and he sensed the same eagerness in Autumn's glances, her curiosity unmistakable. He couldn't wait for the moment when he would finally hand her the sketch, to see her expression and to share that moment they'd been quietly building up to.

The minutes ticked by, and though they didn't speak a word, each shared glance seemed to deepen the connection between them. As the final bell rang, Autumn finally broke the silence, tilting her head toward Kyle with a playful grin. "So, are you going to make that portrait of me today?"

Kyle couldn't help but laugh, shaking his head. "Let me hear you sing first," he replied, raising an eyebrow. "Depending on how good you are, I'll draw you an equally good portrait."

Autumn's eyes sparkled with determination, accepting his challenge with a nod. As the classroom emptied out, the last golden rays of sunlight spilled in through the window, casting a soft glow across the room. She stayed seated at her desk, while Kyle hopped up on her desk, settling in just across from her, eager to witness this side of her.

Autumn took a deep breath, her gaze flickering to him briefly before she began to hum. Kyle recognized the tune almost immediately—it was "Time in a Bottle" by Jim Croce. As she slowly started to sing, her voice filled the room, rich and angelic, each note melting into the next with a delicate, almost haunting beauty.

For Kyle, everything else seemed to fade away. The muffled sounds from the hallway, the distant voices, even the world outside the classroom walls—they all vanished. He found himself entranced, her voice resonating through him, its warmth and emotion pulling him in. He hadn't expected to be so moved, but each word, each note, wrapped around him like a spell. It was as if her voice was painting the very air between them, making time slow down.

As she sang, he couldn't take his eyes off her. The way

the sunlight framed her face, the way her eyes softened as she lost herself in the song—it was a moment he wanted to remember forever. When she finally reached the last line, her voice trailing off with a bittersweet note, she looked up at him, a glimmer of expectation in her eyes.

"How was it?" she asked, her voice barely above a whisper.

Kyle didn't respond right away. He realized there was a dampness at the corner of his eyes, and before he could stop himself, a tear had slipped down his cheek. She paused, taken aback, her expression softening with surprise and concern. "Wait... are you crying?" He quickly brushed at his cheek, smiling as he tried to shrug it off. "It's... it's the wind," he said, glancing toward the window, though they both knew that was just his attempt to save face. Kyle felt something deep within him shift, something he couldn't quite put into words. He was completely captivated by her, as if her voice had unlocked a part of him he didn't know existed. When he finally spoke, his voice was softer than he'd intended. "I'm... I'm just speechless."

Autumn leaned forward, a playful glint still in her eyes, though her expression softened at his serious tone. "So, how was it?" she pressed gently, her curiosity evident.

He hesitated, his gaze dropping as he tried to collect his thoughts. "Can I... tell you later?" he asked, meeting her eyes, hoping she'd understand.

For a moment, she studied his face, and though there was a flicker of disappointment, she nodded. "Alright," she agreed, though her smile held him to his promise. Then, with a mischievous grin, she added, "Now, are you going to draw me or not?"

Kyle chuckled, regaining a bit of his composure. He slung his bag off his shoulder and placed it gently on her desk. "You'll find what you're looking for in there," he said, giving her a small, knowing smile.

Autumn looked from the bag back to him, surprise flashing across her face as she realized he'd already drawn her. She barely had time to say anything before he turned and started walking out of the room, the faint smile still lingering on his lips. She called out a soft "Hey..." but he just raised his hand in a casual wave, not looking back.

Left alone in the empty classroom, Autumn reached for his bag, her fingers brushing its worn edges. She could feel her own heart beating a little faster, realizing that something had just passed between them. Meanwhile, Kyle walked down the hallway, needing a moment to himself to process everything he was feeling.

Autumn's hands trembled slightly as she reached into Kyle's bag, feeling the soft, familiar texture of a rolled canvas beneath her fingertips. She pulled it out, her heart fluttering with anticipation. With bated breath, she carefully unrolled it onto her desk.

The moment she saw it, she gasped. She couldn't look away. The girl on the canvas—herself, but somehow more than herself—seemed to radiate from within. Kyle hadn't just painted a likeness of her; he'd created something transcendent, almost mythical, as though she were a being from some ancient, ethereal realm. In his strokes, she appeared to be bathed in sunlight, each strand of her dark hair catching the golden glow like threads spun from pure light. Her eyes shone in that soft, haunting shade of amber-brown, deep and warm, seeming to hold stories untold.

He had drawn her in that brief, seemingly insignificant moment when she'd turned to thank him by the window. Yet, he'd transformed it, lifting it into something timeless and profound. She could almost feel the breeze he must have imagined, stirring her hair ever so slightly, and the sunlight—so real it felt like it would warm her fingers if she touched it—gently kissing her skin. It was as if he'd captured not only how she looked but also how he saw her, something more vulnerable and sacred than she had ever dared to imagine anyone might see.

Autumn's heart raced as she studied every inch of the painting, realizing that this wasn't a pose she'd held for him, not a moment she'd arranged or expected. He'd drawn her entirely from memory, from details he must have absorbed without her noticing. The thought made her pulse quicken, a blush creeping up her cheeks. She felt as though she were peering into his heart, glimpsing something he'd kept hidden even from himself.

It was overwhelming, seeing herself like this—as if through the eyes of someone who found her not just beautiful, but magical, a person worth capturing in a moment of quiet wonder. She was struck by the depth of his gaze, by how much of her he'd truly seen, and for the first time, she felt completely understood.

Autumn's fingers lingered on the edge of the canvas, her chest tight with emotions she couldn't name. There was a power in this image, a beauty that felt like it had been waiting forever to be discovered. She realized now, with her heart beating like a wild drum, that this was more than just a portrait; it was an expression of something rare, something beyond words. And in that moment, she felt herself drawn to Kyle in a way she'd never felt before, as though he'd uncovered a part of her she'd never known was there.

Kyle made his way to the practice field, his mind spinning, his heart heavy with an ache he couldn't quite place. The flood of emotions he felt after leaving Autumn was almost too much to bear; he needed space, a moment to breathe, to make sense of it all. He barely noticed his friends gathering around him, calling his name as they readied for practice. He just needed to push it all aside, if only for a little while.

As they started warm-ups, he glanced up, instinctively, toward the art room window. And there she was—Autumn. She was watching him from above, her hand resting on the iron window grill. Though they were far apart, he felt the intensity of her gaze as if she were right beside him. Her face held an unreadable expression, one he couldn't quite decipher from this distance. There was something poignant in the way she looked down at him, as if she, too, was grappling with everything that had transpired between them.

Kyle quickly looked away, pretending he hadn't seen her. He focused on his practice, throwing himself into each drill with an almost desperate energy, trying to ground himself. But her image lingered at the edge of his mind, unshakable. Every pass, every sprint, every routine felt laced with her presence, as if she were there, watching, a silent specter of his own emotions. When practice finally ended, he barely paused to chat with his friends. He just muttered a quick goodbye and rushed home, feeling the weight of the day press down on him. He barely ate dinner, mumbling a few words to his mom, then retreated to his room. In the quiet solitude of his room, lying in bed, all the moments of the day replayed in his mind on a relentless loop—the way she'd looked at the portrait, the look they'd shared from the window, her voice lingering in his memory.

He closed his eyes, yet her image was there, vivid and haunting. Eventually, exhaustion took over, and Kyle drifted into a restless sleep, carrying with him the strange and beautiful weight of his feelings for Autumn.

The next day arrived, and the tension between Kyle and Autumn was almost tangible. Neither of them felt ready to face the other, but fate had drawn them together in that quiet classroom. Kyle slipped into his seat beside her, his heart pounding as he stared down at his notebook. There was a silence, thick with unsaid words and unacknowledged emotions. He couldn't take it any longer.

Without looking at her, he asked softly, "So... did you like the painting?"

For a moment, there was no reply. Then, he dared to look over at her. Autumn's eyes were glistening, a tear caught at the edge of her lashes. She looked down, trying to hold herself together, her voice wavering as she whispered, "Thank you so much, Kyle. I've never received anything like this before... It means a lot."

Kyle's heart twisted. Seeing her this moved, this vulnerable, made him realize just how much his gesture had affected her. The sincerity in her words, the tremor in her voice—this was no ordinary thank you. It felt like a piece of himself, offered and received, connecting them in a way words could never express.

He gently murmured, “It’s okay. I’m just... I’m glad you liked it.”

But deep down, he felt something shifting, something falling into place within him. He couldn’t name it, but he knew he would hold onto this moment, the memory of her tear-streaked smile, forever.

The rest of the day passed in a blur. They exchanged glances throughout the classes, each look holding a silent acknowledgment of the bond they had now. When the final bell rang, Kyle gathered his things and was about to leave when he heard her call his name. He turned to see her standing there, her face flushed with a soft, pink warmth.
“Thank you so much,” she said again, this time with a smile—a real, radiant smile that lit up her whole face.
Kyle’s own smile grew, and he replied, “I’m really happy you liked it.” And with one last glance, he walked away, feeling lighter and fuller than he’d ever felt before.
It felt as if Kyle had found a new rhythm to his life, a melody he wanted to wake up to each day. Every morning held the quiet thrill of anticipation—seeing her, talking to her, and just feeling her presence nearby. Every word he spoke now felt like it was meant to make her smile, and every laugh he shared seemed like it was worth more than any laughter he’d known before. Time slipped by unnoticed, and weekends, which had once been a welcome escape, now felt like

interruptions. All he could think about was how much he looked forward to Monday.

Two weeks passed in this daze, each day bringing him closer to her. And then, on one Monday morning, as he entered the art class, he found Autumn looking uncharacteristically upset. She sat at her desk, arms folded and cheeks puffed up in an almost comical show of annoyance. Her brows were drawn down, and her lips were pressed into a pout, her whole expression radiating a kind of stubborn frustration that was both funny and oddly endearing. Kyle couldn't help but laugh. "What happened?" he asked, moving closer to her and reaching out to poke one of her puffed-up cheeks. She swatted his hand playfully but let out a huff, rolling her eyes. "One of the professors told me off for talking too much in class," she said, glancing at him with wide, indignant eyes. "Can you believe it? Me, scolded for just... talking?" She looked up at him with a wounded expression, clearly waiting for sympathy.

He chuckled, feigning surprise. "No way—you talk too much?" His tone was teasing, his smile wide. She looked up at him, still pouting, and then with a little smirk, added, "Well, yes, but still. How could anyone scold this innocent face?" She raised her chin slightly, as if daring him to disagree, her eyes sparkling with humor beneath her feigned irritation.

Kyle grinned, his heart racing a little as he pretended to study her face, his expression playful.

"Hmm, innocent, huh?" he mused, tapping his chin dramatically. But she saw the teasing glint in his eyes and couldn't hold back her laughter anymore, her mock anger melting away as they both cracked up, their laughter echoing through the nearly empty classroom.

He couldn't stop staring at her as she laughed, her shoulders shaking, her eyes shining. Time felt like it slowed to a crawl in that moment, everything else fading into the background. There was a grace to her even in her frustration, a lightness he couldn't put into words. Her happiness had somehow become the most precious thing in the world to him, and he found himself captivated by even the smallest details—the curve of her smile, the way her nose crinkled slightly as she giggled, the pinkish glow of her cheeks.

The rest of the class seemed to slip by in an instant as they playfully bantered, both of them caught up in the warmth and ease of their connection. And as the class drew to a close, Kyle took a deep breath, gathering up his courage.

"Hey, would you... like to meet my friends sometime?" he asked, his voice softer than usual, his gaze searching her face for a reaction.

Autumn's eyes widened a little, and she looked down, an uncertain smile forming on her lips. She bit her lip, hesitating for a moment, as if weighing the idea.

But when she glanced back up and caught the hopeful look in his eyes, her smile softened. "Alright," she said with a slight nod, her voice barely above a whisper. "Tomorrow, then." Her answer sent a wave of warmth through him, and he barely managed to contain his excitement. "Tomorrow it is," he replied, his smile growing, feeling like the luckiest guy in the world.

They exchanged one last smile before she turned to leave, and Kyle was left with a sense of anticipation he hadn't felt in a long time. Tomorrow couldn't come soon enough.

Kyle made his way quickly to the locker room to meet up with the guys. As soon as he saw them, he leaned in and said, "Hey, let's catch up after practice, alright?"

Sam immediately shot him a knowing look, clearly understanding Kyle's intentions. Ryder raised an eyebrow, a smirk creeping across his face. "Oh? Finally deciding to hang out with us lowly friends, huh?" he teased, crossing his arms and giving Kyle a mock-serious look. Kyle rolled his eyes and laughed, deciding to go along with the sarcasm. "Yeah, yeah. Gotta balance my busy social calendar somehow."

As practice wrapped up, the group headed to a small shop a few blocks away with a couple of benches and a row of bikes parked out front. They each grabbed a drink and settled down, some perched on the benches and others leaning against their bikes, the familiar scenery giving them a sense of ease.

Kyle took a deep breath and looked around at them, realizing just how much he'd missed these casual hangouts. Clearing his throat, he began, "So, as you guys might've noticed, I haven't exactly been around much lately."

Ryan snorted. "Oh, trust us. We've noticed," he said, grinning. Kyle chuckled but pressed on, feeling a bit of nerves creeping up as he continued. "Well, there's a reason for that. I... I met this girl, Autumn."

The group fell silent, their eyes widening with interest. Kyle started to describe Autumn to them, painting a picture of her with such vivid detail that even he surprised himself. He told them about her smile, her laughter, the way she saw the world with this unique curiosity and depth. He even told them about the portrait he'd drawn of her and how it had moved her. He felt a warmth spreading through him as he spoke, like every word was just pouring out from someplace deep within. As he finished, Ryder let out a low whistle. "Damn, man," he said, nudging Kyle with his elbow. "You've got it bad." Sam, who'd been listening with a quiet smile, leaned forward, his voice soft but certain. "You love her, don't you?"

The question hung in the air, and for a moment, Kyle felt like the ground had shifted under him. Love? He hadn't quite thought of it that way. It wasn't just a simple word, and somehow, it felt too small to contain all the feelings he had for her. He searched for words, struggling to express himself. "It's... different," he said finally, his voice thoughtful. "Love doesn't seem like enough, you know? It's... it's more than that. I feel like I want to protect her like a brother, care for her like a mother, listen to her like a best friend. It's this mix of everything, and I can't put a label on it."

The others exchanged glances, nodding, sensing the depth of what he was feeling. For a moment, there was a comfortable silence as they sipped their drinks, letting the weight of Kyle's words sink in.
Kyle finally broke the silence with a small, almost wistful smile. "Love, huh..." he murmured, more to himself than to them, as if he was testing the word, feeling its edges. He let the thought trail off, not wanting to dig too deep, and gave a slight shrug. "Anyway," he said, shifting the topic back to their usual banter, "let's head home."

They rode off together, the wind cool on their faces as the sun began to set, but Kyle's mind stayed on Autumn the whole way home, the word love lingering on his mind like an unfinished melody. The next day, Kyle found himself sitting beside Autumn in class, his mind wandering in that familiar way it always did when he grew close to someone. He had this habit—this almost unconscious drive—to peel back the layers of a person's thoughts, asking them questions that delved into who they truly were. Today, he couldn't resist starting up one of those conversations with Autumn.

"Hey," he said, his voice low, almost hesitant. "Do you... believe in God?" Autumn looked at him, slightly taken aback. "Why do you ask?" she replied, a curious smile dancing on her lips.

Kyle shrugged, feeling a bit self-conscious but pressing forward. "I guess I just wanted to know your perspective on it. You know, where you stand with... bigger things."

Autumn tilted her head thoughtfully before answering, her expression softening. "Yes, I completely believe in God. Fate and God are the two things that keep me grounded," she said, her voice holding a certain reverence. "I feel like they're connected, like they guide us through life, even if we can't always see it."

Kyle listened, letting her words settle over him. He admired the certainty in her voice, the way she spoke with conviction, as though she'd come to terms with these ideas a long time ago. He, on the other hand, felt that familiar tug of uncertainty—a feeling he'd been carrying for as long as he could remember.

Autumn noticed the pensive look on his face and tilted her head a bit closer, studying him. "What about you? Do you believe in God?" she asked gently, almost as if she didn't want to break his train of thought.

Kyle looked down at his hands, thinking carefully. "I don't know," he admitted. "I'm still... on the edge, I guess. Sometimes, I feel like there's something out there, something bigger than us. Other times, I'm not so sure. It's like I'm waiting for a sign, something to push me one way or the other."

Autumn gave him a gentle smile, as if understanding that feeling of being caught in between. "I get that," she said softly. "Sometimes faith isn't about knowing; it's about trusting even when you don't have all the answers."

Her words lingered with him, stirring something deep inside that he couldn't quite place. He felt as though he'd just uncovered another hidden piece of her, and in doing so, he'd glimpsed a part of himself too. For the rest of the class, he found himself stealing glances at her, thoughts of faith and fate mingling with the warmth of their conversation, leaving him with a sense of quiet awe at how she seemed to see the world.

Kyle hesitated a moment, looking out the window as he gathered his thoughts. He wanted to ask something deeper, something that had been on his mind since his conversation with Autumn about fate and destiny. Her certainty on these topics fascinated him, but also left him feeling unsettled in a way he couldn't quite explain.

Turning back to her, he asked, "So... if there's something you really want—something you'd do anything for—would you just leave it up to fate if it didn't come easily? Would you believe that maybe it just wasn't meant to be?"

Autumn considered his question, her gaze growing introspective. "Well... yeah. I think so. If it's fated for you to have it, then it'll come to you. No matter what. But if it's not in your fate, then no matter how much you try, it just won't happen." Her words hung in the air, their simplicity somehow both comforting and frustrating. Kyle took them in, but they didn't sit easily with him. The idea of accepting limits felt almost foreign—like giving up. For him, if he truly wanted something, he would go after it with everything he had. To him, fate was something he could bend with enough effort.

He managed a nod, though it was clear from his expression that he was turning over her answer in his mind. "I get that," he said slowly. "But... I don't know. I think, if there's something I care about that deeply, I'd want to try everything to make it happen. Even if it's not 'meant to be,' I'd want to give it a shot." Autumn smiled softly, recognizing the resolve in his eyes. "I can see that about you," she replied, her voice gentle. "I think it's a beautiful way to see things... fighting for what you want. I guess maybe that's what makes us different. I'm just a little more... I don't know, willing to let things go." They sat in silence for a few moments, each wrapped in their own thoughts. To Kyle, Autumn's perspective felt both foreign and strangely intriguing—her calm acceptance of fate contrasting sharply with his own desire to shape his future, to resist anything that threatened what he valued. A few minutes later, breaking the pensive silence, he asked her, "So... you ready to meet my friends?"

Autumn looked at him, her eyes lighting up with curiosity. There was no hesitation—just a spark of interest as she thought about meeting the people Kyle spent his time with. She gave him a playful smile and nodded. "Yeah, okay. I'd like that. I'm curious to finally see what your friends are like." He grinned, relieved and excited, and they gathered their things before heading to the ground where his friends waited. As they walked, Kyle's heart raced with a mix of anticipation and nerves. This was more than just an introduction—he wanted Autumn to see a part of his world, a part of him he hadn't shared with anyone quite like this before.

Kyle led Autumn over to a bench near the field, gesturing for her to sit comfortably. "Wait here," he said with a reassuring smile. "I'll bring the guys over." She nodded, her curiosity about his friends growing with each step he took away.

He crossed the field, his eyes scanning for his group. Sam, who had been stretching nearby, spotted him approaching and immediately knew something was up. "So," Sam said with a smirk, "are we finally meeting her?"

Kyle just chuckled, waving him over without a word. He spotted Ryan and Ryder, who were kicking around a soccer ball a little further off, and Nate was by his usual spot, reading on a bench. "Guys, come on," Kyle called out, motioning them to gather up. "I've got someone for you to meet."

Ryan raised an eyebrow, exchanging a knowing glance with Ryder, who gave a low whistle. "It's happening, huh?" Ryan said, grinning as he followed Kyle's lead. Nate, a bit more oblivious, looked up with curiosity, tucked his book away, and trailed behind. As they walked across the field, Ryder joked, "About time you introduced us to this mystery girl, man." Kyle just rolled his eyes, not offering any answers.

When they reached the bench where Autumn was waiting, Kyle felt his heart pick up a beat. He introduced each of his friends in turn, starting with Sam, who gave a small, confident wave. "Sam's the humor of the group," Kyle said with a grin. "But you'll have to look past his humor; it's an acquired taste." Autumn laughed softly, and Sam gave her an amused nod. "I promise I'm mostly harmless," he joked, flashing a playful grin.

Next, Kyle introduced Ryan. "Ryan here's the one who'll remember everyone's birthday, even if we forget our own," he said, giving his friend an appreciative nudge. "Kind of the heart of the group."

Ryan smiled warmly at Autumn and gave a friendly wave. "Nice to meet you, Autumn. You've got a cool name, by the way." Ryder was next, standing with an easy confidence. "And this is Ryder," Kyle said. "You'll catch him beatboxing or talking about his latest idea."

Ryder smirked, giving her a nod. "Glad we finally get to meet you. Kyle's talked about you enough for us to wonder if you're real," he teased, earning a quiet chuckle from Autumn. Finally, Nate stepped up, looking a bit unsure but smiling anyway. "And this is Nate," Kyle said, giving him a quick pat on the back. "The brains of the group, keeps us grounded—and probably the only one here who can find his way out of a paper bag without getting lost." Nate blushed slightly, chuckling as he said, "Hey, if you ever want a tour of the campus, I'm your guy."

Autumn's face lit up with genuine amusement, clearly taken by their different personalities. "It's nice meeting you all," she said warmly. "You're definitely not what I expected...in a good way," she added, glancing at Kyle with a little smile. "Stick around, and you'll see just how weird we all are," Sam quipped, making her laugh.

“Yeah, you should hang out with us sometime,” Ryan added, his friendly gaze making her feel instantly welcomed. Ryder and Nate nodded in agreement, each of them giving her a little smile.
After a few more lighthearted exchanges, the guys headed off to practice, but Kyle hung back with Autumn for a moment. “So?” he asked, eager to hear her thoughts. “What did you think?” She took a moment, glancing over at them as they warmed up on the field. “They're...actually pretty great,” she said, smiling. “I didn't expect them to be so friendly—or so funny.”

Hearing that, Kyle felt a weight lift. “I'm glad you liked them,” he said, his voice softer than usual. “They mean a lot to me. And now...” He paused, his words trailing off. “Now, I'm glad you've met them.”

She gave him a look, her smile warmer than ever. “I can tell they mean a lot to you, Kyle.” He nodded, feeling a deep sense of gratitude he couldn't quite put into words. After saying goodbye, he turned back toward the field, but not without stealing one last glance at her. As he joined his friends, he felt a deep satisfaction, as if everything he cared about was somehow finally coming together.

As the days rolled closer to the cultural fest, an energy buzzed through the campus, with preparations in full swing. Kyle remembered Nate's earlier suggestion about the science project competition, and so, one afternoon, he gathered everyone together. "Alright, guys, let's do this science competition Nate's been talking about," Kyle said, nudging Nate as he spoke.

Nate grinned, pushing up his glasses. "Finally! I've got a few ideas we can start with," he said, launching into a detailed plan. The group listened, nodding in agreement as Nate mapped out a project, each of them chiming in with suggestions. Even Ryan, who usually hung back in group decisions, seemed to get swept up in the excitement, throwing in a few ideas.

With everyone onboard, the group dove into work, setting a schedule for their practices and project work. Between that and the many other events, the days became packed. Kyle found himself balancing practice, project meetings, and helping Nate coordinate. On top of that, his ongoing rivalry with Alex flared up as they both competed for the best spot on the football team.

Autumn, too, was deeply immersed in her own preparations. She'd been selected to sing during the performance the art class would be putting on, so she was practicing tirelessly, staying after class to rehearse and hone each note. When Kyle passed by her classroom, he often heard her soft, angelic voice drifting through the hallway, but their schedules rarely lined up for them to talk.

Days passed in this whirlwind, and soon, a whole week had gone by with just brief hellos exchanged between them in the halls. Kyle found himself missing their easy conversations and her warm laughter, but he figured she was just as tied up as he was. Finally, on a Friday afternoon, he managed to catch her outside the classroom, still packing up her things.

"Hey, Autumn," he called out, his voice just loud enough to grab her attention.

She turned to him, a tired smile lighting up her face. "Hey, Kyle! It's been a while," she said, slipping her bag over her shoulder.

"Yeah, it has," he replied with a chuckle. There was a moment of silence, then Kyle's face lit up with an idea. "Listen... I want to show you something tomorrow," he said, his eyes shining with a hint of mystery.

Her curiosity was piqued instantly. "Oh? What is it?" she asked, looking at him with an intrigued smile.

Kyle just shrugged, his smile widening. "You'll have to see for yourself," he replied, his tone playful. He could tell she was intrigued, and he liked that he'd managed to stir her curiosity. Without hesitation, Autumn nodded. "Alright, I'm in. Just tell me when and where," she said, her tone equally lighthearted.

He nodded, a bit relieved, and said, "Great. I'll pick you up tomorrow." He didn't give her any more hints, and Autumn didn't press him further, trusting that whatever he had planned would be worth the wait.
As he joined his friends for practice, his mind buzzed with anticipation, and he couldn't wait to show Autumn the surprise he had in store for her.

Kyle woke up the next morning with excitement in his chest. Today was the day he'd finally get to show Autumn the treehouse—a special place that only he and his friends knew about. He'd been looking forward to sharing it with her, knowing she'd appreciate the secret and the beauty of the place.

After breakfast, he went to the garage to clean up his bike, wiping down every corner and tightening anything that needed it. His mom came over to check on him, noticing his obvious anticipation.

"Meeting up with friends today?" she asked with a knowing smile.

Kyle nodded, trying to seem casual. "Yeah, we're just going to hang out somewhere special."

His mom gave him a thoughtful look, glancing out the window. "Better take your jacket. Looks like it might rain," she advised, handing him his worn leather jacket.

"Thanks, Mom," he said, shrugging it on and adjusting the collar. He felt prepared—almost like he was going on a small adventure. He couldn't help but imagine the look on Autumn's face when she saw the treehouse for the first time. It was hidden away in a spot so tranquil, surrounded by trees and overlooking a view that felt like it was straight out of a storybook. The place was simple but magical in its own way, just like she was.

The ride to Autumn's place felt like it flew by as his thoughts swirled with anticipation. When he pulled up, he slowed to take in her house, noticing things he hadn't paid much attention to before. Her home matched her personality perfectly: a little cottage that exuded warmth and charm. The walls were painted a pale blue, slightly faded by time, and surrounded by a garden that was somehow both wild and beautiful. Delicate flowers grew in every color imaginable, spilling over in small patches along the pathway and up toward the windows, giving the house a whimsical, fairytale feel. It was clear someone took care of the garden with love, just as Autumn nurtured everything and everyone she came across. A small, weathered bench sat beneath a sprawling tree, with a few stray leaves drifting down from its branches, painting the ground in autumn colors. Near the door, a delicate wind chime hung, tinkling softly in the morning breeze. The house felt like a world unto itself, private yet open to anyone who wanted to find peace within its bounds.

As Kyle pulled up and settled his bike in front of Autumn's house, he took a quick look at his watch, making sure he wasn't too early. His heart raced a bit, wondering what she'd think of the treehouse and the plan he had in mind. He'd never brought anyone there outside of his closest friends—it was special, a part of himself he was about to share with her.

Autumn opened the door and stepped out onto the path, catching sight of him leaning casually against his bike, the morning light casting a warm glow over him. He looked effortlessly cool in his leather jacket, his hair a little tousled by the ride. She felt her cheeks flush as she took in the sight. There was something about seeing him here, just waiting for her, that made her heart skip a beat.

For a moment, she hesitated on the path, smoothing down her scarf as if it might help her keep her composure. She forced herself to walk toward him, though each step made the little flutter in her chest feel stronger. He noticed her approach and smiled, his face lighting up in a way that made her own smile grow, her blush deepening. There was a warmth in his gaze, a quiet gentleness that made her feel like she was the only person in the world he saw at that moment.

"Hey," she greeted him, trying to keep her voice steady, though a smile tugged at her lips. "Morning," he replied, holding out the helmet. "Ready for an adventure?"

As she took the helmet from him, their fingers brushed, sending a slight spark through her hand. She felt her cheeks grow warmer and looked down for a second, hoping he wouldn't notice. But he did, and a faint smirk played at the corners of his mouth.

"What's with the blush?" he asked playfully, leaning a little closer. She could feel her face grow even warmer. "It's just... you look different today," she replied, stumbling slightly over her words. "Good different," she added quickly, realizing she was dangerously close to rambling.

"Well, glad to hear it." Kyle chuckled, looking both pleased and amused as he handed her the helmet. "Let's get going before I turn red too." Autumn laughed, feeling more at ease as she adjusted the helmet and climbed onto the bike behind him. She wrapped her arms around his waist, feeling the solidness of his back as she settled in. It felt natural, comforting even, to hold onto him like this. He glanced back over his shoulder, giving her a quick smile, and then they were off, the gentle rumble of the engine blending with the cool morning air. As they rode through winding paths and the trees began to thicken, Autumn's heart raced in excitement. She leaned her head slightly against his shoulder, taking in the moment. With each mile, she found herself relaxing, feeling the thrill of the ride but also feeling undeniably safe with him.

They were on their way to something special, she could tell, but she was in no hurry for the journey to end. As they climbed higher, clouds began to drift in thickening waves overhead, casting a soft gray over the landscape. It only made the rich greens of the trees and hills pop even more, creating a picture-perfect view of Orange's natural beauty. Autumn couldn't help but marvel at the way the misty atmosphere enhanced everything, like the world itself was painted in delicate strokes just for them. She gripped Kyle's waist a little tighter, feeling the rush of the ride and the thrill of the unknown.

Kyle leaned back slightly, his voice raised to cut through the wind. "Any guesses on where we're headed?" he asked. She shook her head, laughing. "Not a clue. But... this path goes to the hill where the university is, right?"

Kyle grinned, his eyes briefly flicking back at her. "Good guess. But we're going beyond that. There's a spot on the other side, something special. You'll see." Curiosity sparked in her eyes, and she leaned a bit closer. "What kind of spot?" He just chuckled, giving a little shake of his head. "Patience, Autumn. It'll be worth the wait," he replied, speeding up as a light drizzle began to fall, the tiny droplets cool on their skin. The slight acceleration made her instinctively hold onto him tighter, her heart skipping a beat as she clung to him, trusting him fully.

The air grew cooler as they continued uphill, the sound of the bike's engine reverberating through the trees as they passed. With each bend in the path, the landscape changed, the view expanding into vast stretches of forest and rolling hills below. She felt like they were climbing into a world of their own, far from the usual scenes of town life. Then, just as the drizzle began to thicken, he slowed down and pointed ahead, his voice tinged with excitement. "Look up there."

Autumn's gaze followed his finger, and her breath caught in her throat. There, nestled high up and partially hidden among the dense trees, was a treehouse like something out of a dream. It was rustic and charming, suspended between two massive trees, with branches woven around it like nature itself was guarding the place. Wooden planks formed a pathway leading to it, and she could see the faint outline of windows, reflecting the soft, diffused light filtering through the clouds.

"Wow..." she murmured, her voice barely audible as she took it all in. She hadn't seen anything like it. It was a secret world tucked away from everything else, untouched and hidden. Kyle smiled, seeing her awe. He revved the engine slightly, closing the last bit of distance between them and the base of the treehouse. As they parked beneath it, Autumn remained speechless, her gaze fixed upward. She was transfixed, looking up at the wooden structure nestled between thick branches, as if it were a magical place far from the everyday world. Kyle climbed off the bike and stood beside her, a satisfied smile on his face as he watched her take it all in.

This..." she started, finally finding her voice. "Kyle, this is beautiful. I don't even have words." He looked at her, his own expression softening. "I figured you'd like it. Only my friends and I know about this place. It's... special." She nodded, still stunned as she took in every detail. The treehouse felt like something out of a fairytale, yet somehow, it also felt like it was meant just for them in this moment. The drizzle was growing heavier, making the leaves glisten, and she could smell the fresh, earthy scent of rain mixing with the rich wood around them. "Ready to go up?" he asked, holding out his hand.

She took it, He helped her climb the path to the treehouse. As they reached the platform, she turned, taking in the breathtaking view of the hills below, now shrouded in mist, stretching as far as her eyes could see. It was like standing on top of the world, with nothing but nature and Kyle by her side. As Autumn took in the sight of the treehouse, her eyes sparkled with amazement. She seemed almost transported, her gaze sweeping over every corner of the hidden sanctuary. Kyle, watching her, couldn't help but feel a sense of pride and warmth—it was a part of his world that he hadn't shared with anyone outside his group of friends, and here she was, completely captivated. "Ready to go inside?" he asked, giving her shoulder a gentle tap. She nodded, her smile growing as they opened the door together.

The inside was cozy and inviting, a blend of rugged charm and lived-in warmth. The walls were decorated with photos of Kyle and his friends, snapshots of their adventures, capturing laughter, surprise, and genuine moments. The smell of old wood and faint hints of oil and leather filled the air, mixing with the earthy scent that had wafted in from outside. Bike parts were neatly piled in a corner—a testament to all the times they'd tinkered with things here. A few mismatched sofas and armchairs sat around a low table, and a makeshift shelf held books, a few snacks, and random knickknacks that each held a memory. Autumn walked slowly, studying each photo as if she could glimpse pieces of his past through them. She pointed to a particular photo of the whole group, standing outside the treehouse, arms thrown over each other's shoulders, grinning like kids on their first adventure. "When was this taken?" she asked. Kyle joined her gaze. "That was the first time we all came here together. Nate found this place, actually. We cleaned it up, made it ours," he said, his voice softening with nostalgia.

She moved around the room, asking about everything she found—a book on the shelf with a worn spine, a beat-up jacket slung over the arm of a chair, a small model bike tucked between the pillows on the sofa. Kyle answered every question, happy that she was taking such an interest in his world, in the pieces of his life that most people never saw.

Finally, she paused and looked at him, her eyes alight with excitement. Kyle had been watching her the entire time, barely able to contain the emotions rising within him. She looked perfect here, as though she belonged in this space that held so many memories. He settled back into the sofa, his heart full, feeling like he'd shared something profound without needing words. Just being there, watching her take it all in, felt like one of those small, perfect moments he'd never forget.

Kyle and Autumn spent the next hour while simply goofing around in the treehouse, sharing laughs and teasing each other. They uncovered random items his friends had stashed here over the years, and each new discovery made her smile grow a little wider, making Kyle's heart swell. But then, the distant rumble of thunder rolled in, and soon, rain began to patter softly against the window, a gentle rhythm that quickly turned into a steady downpour. Autumn wandered over to the window, resting both hands on the sill and leaning forward slightly to look outside. Her eyes widened in wonder as she watched the rain dance across the trees and ground below. "It's beautiful, isn't it?" she murmured, her voice barely above a whisper, completely lost in the scene before her.

Kyle, leaning against the window beside her, felt himself caught not by the view outside, but by how her eyes reflected it. She was captivated, her gaze filled with a simple joy that made everything outside look more vivid, more alive. He nodded, his voice soft, "Yes, it's beautiful indeed." But to him, it wasn't the rain or the view—it was seeing it all through her eyes, as if she brought a new life to everything she looked at. Autumn turned her head to find him watching her, a gentle smile tugging at her lips. "Why are you looking at me like that?" she laughed, her eyes bright with curiosity. Kyle shrugged, a playful smile dancing on his face. "Nothing," he replied, but his eyes said everything he couldn't put into words. She just shook her head, still smiling, and slipped off her scarf, tossing it onto the sofa. "Come on, let's go outside and enjoy the rain properly!" she said, her excitement infectious.

Without hesitation, they climbed down from the treehouse and made their way to a familiar spot where Sam often stood, flinging rocks down the hillside for fun. "This is where Sam usually throws rocks from," Kyle said, motioning toward the ledge. But Autumn wasn't interested in rocks. She stepped forward, letting the rain pour down around her, her arms stretching out like a child embracing a new world. She twirled slowly, letting the drops splash against her face, her laughter blending with the rhythm of the rain. She looked completely carefree; her happiness so pure it seemed to dissolve every worry in the air.

Kyle stood back for a moment, taking in the sight of her, her joy filling him with a warmth that had nothing to do with the summer air. The way she embraced the rain reminded him of how precious and childlike she was, a rare mix of innocence and courage. It was a side of her he wanted to protect, something he'd come to cherish in the deepest parts of his heart. He walked closer, rain soaking him too now, but he didn't mind. Right then, there was nowhere else he wanted to be and no one else he'd rather be with.

As Autumn continued to spin and laugh under the rain, Kyle couldn't help but call out, "Hey, be careful! You're going to catch a cold if you stay out here too long!" His voice was tinged with worry, but she just laughed, waving him off. "You worry way too much," she teased, but her laughter softened when she finally stepped back under the shelter of the tree. She looked down at herself, sighing lightly. "Ugh, my makeup is ruined... I spent so much time on it this morning," she said, sounding a bit regretful. She poked at her cheek with a frown, "Look at this pimple. How do I even look now?"

Kyle leaned in slightly, just close enough to see the small detail she was fussing over. "Hey..." he said softly, his voice carrying a warmth that made her glance up. "You're the most beautiful girl I've ever met, Autumn. Those little things—your so-called 'imperfections'—they only make you more beautiful."

Autumn's eyes widened as his words sank in, her cheeks flushing a deep pink that was only partly from the cold rain. She looked down, shy and a little overwhelmed, not sure how to respond. After a second, she gave him a gentle push, trying to hide her blush. "You really say too much, you know that?" Kyle chuckled, watching her dart back toward the tree, a playful smile tugging at his lips. As she leaned against the trunk, trying to dry herself off, he couldn't help but smile at the sight, his heart melting by the quiet happiness of the moment. As they waited for the rain to slow, Kyle couldn't resist one last tease. He leaned in with a playful smile and said, "You know, they say a butterfly can not see its own wings."

Autumn's face turned a shade deeper, catching his meaning immediately. She let out a flustered sigh, her hands coming up in defense as she tried to keep her composure. "Oh, stop it, Kyle," she muttered, half-laughing, her cheeks glowing. He grinned but finally relented, laughing softly as he promised, "Alright, alright, I'll stop." They shared a quiet smile as the rain began to lighten, leaving only a gentle mist falling around them. The air felt fresh and peaceful, and there was a stillness between them, a soft silence that felt full of meaning, as though they didn't need words to feel connected. After a moment, Kyle glanced at the sky, realizing the late hour. "We should probably get going. I'll drop you home before it gets dark," he said gently.

Autumn nodded, and they made their way to his bike. She climbed on behind him, slipping her arms around his waist without a word. The entire ride downhill was filled with a comforting silence, her head lightly resting against his back, her grip firm yet gentle. Neither of them spoke, yet it felt like they shared more in those quiet moments than they had all day.

Finally, they reached her house. Autumn dismounted slowly, a small smile playing on her lips as she looked up at him. Leaning close, she whispered, "Thank you, Kyle." The words were barely audible, but the warmth in her voice was unmistakable. She turned, glancing back one last time before heading inside. Kyle watched her go, his heart full, feeling as though he'd spent the day in a dream. As he drove home, he couldn't get her out of his mind—how genuine she was, her laugh, her shyness. She was perfect, he thought to himself, and he knew he'd do anything to keep her safe, to keep her smiling.

At home, over dinner, his mom noticed his glowing expression. "You look unusually happy tonight, Kyle," she remarked with a knowing smile.

He simply laughed, brushing it off. "I'll tell you later, Mom," he said, unable to stop smiling. As he lay down that night, drifting to sleep, his mind replayed the day over and over, filling his thoughts with her.

The next day was Sunday, but even as he went about his routine, his thoughts were only on her. He felt an energy, an inspiration, one that made him pick up his pen and start writing again. With her in his life, he felt like he had found the spark he needed for his book. Yet all he truly wanted was for Monday to arrive, so he could see her again.

Monday morning, Kyle and his friends moved as a group towards the registration hall for the science project competition, Nate practically bouncing with excitement. "I still can't believe you all agreed to this," he said with a grin, looking at each of them.

"Well, don't get too excited," Ryder teased, giving Nate a friendly nudge. "We're only doing it because you wouldn't stop asking." Nate rolled his eyes, grinning back. "As if! You'll be thanking me when we win. This is going to be epic, guys!"

Ryan chimed in, "If we come up with anything that doesn't involve heavy math or physics, I'll be impressed."
As they entered the registration hall, the team learned that the theme for the project was "Innovative Solutions for Societal Impact." They'd need to create something meaningful that could make a positive difference in people's lives. "Alright, so how do we feel about this?" Kyle asked as they moved to a quieter corner to brainstorm.

Sam shrugged. “Not my usual thing, but I’m game. Besides, we’ve already got Nate doing all the thinking, right?”

Nate shot him a mock glare. “Hey, I want everyone’s ideas here! Sam, that means even yours.” He glanced around, looking expectant. “So... any thoughts?” They brainstormed for a while, each of them throwing ideas into the mix. “What if we did something environmental?” Ryan suggested. “Like, something that could reduce pollution or help recycling?”

“I like it,” Kyle nodded. “But it has to be something practical.” Ryder, who’d been listening thoughtfully, leaned forward. “Or maybe it could be a tech solution that helps people connect—maybe some kind of app for community service?”

“Nice,” Kyle said, intrigued. “We can brainstorm more on that tomorrow. Let’s pick the best one after we’ve thought them through.” Between science project planning and football practices, their schedules were packed, but there was a palpable energy in the group, a sense that they were all working towards something meaningful.

Meanwhile, Autumn was just as busy, practicing with her art class. Each day after classes, she and Kyle would meet up in a quiet spot, catching up on the day’s activities. As they sat on a low stone wall one evening, Kyle asked, "So, how's the singing practice coming along?" Autumn laughed, brushing a loose strand of hair from her face. "Oh, you know. Intense. Our instructor keeps saying I have to 'bring the emotion.' She's a perfectionist!"

Kyle smiled. "I'm sure you'll nail it. You've got that... I don't know, passion or something." Autumn raised an eyebrow playfully. "Or something?" He chuckled. "You know what I mean. Can't wait to see you on stage."

They sat quietly for a moment, watching the last rays of sunlight filter through the trees. Later in the week, they met again to finalize their plans for the science project and checked the festival schedule together. When Kyle read it aloud, the lineup was clear:

- **Day 1:** Art class performance.
- **Day 2:** Science project competition.
- **Day 3:** The football match.

"Autumn, you're going to crush that stage," Kyle said, a hint of pride in his voice. "Day 1's all about you." She smiled, nudging him lightly. "And Day 3 is all about you." Nate clapped his hands together. "Alright, team. Let's make this the best festival week ever." Sam smirked. "I'm just here to see all of you get nervous." Ryder groaned, but there was a glint of excitement in his eyes. “Well, bring it on. I want a good challenge.” In that moment, Kyle felt a deep gratitude for the people around him. They were about to dive into an unforgettable week, and he was ready for every second of it. The week had been nothing short of a whirlwind for Kyle and his friends. They finally found a solid concept for their science project: a compact water filtration device that could be used in rural areas with limited access to clean drinking water. Nate was thrilled, practically vibrating with excitement as he gathered them around during lunch to discuss the technical details.

“I mean, guys,” Nate enthused, barely able to contain himself, “we’re talking about a filtration system that could be portable and solar-powered, something that could really make a difference. Imagine getting this idea out there for real!” Kyle, intrigued, leaned forward. “And you think we can actually pull this off in time for the fest?” Nate nodded confidently. “If everyone does their part, yeah. I’ve already drafted the initial design. Ryder, I’ll need you to help with the presentation slides — we need them to look impressive. And Ryan, you’re good with hands-on stuff, so you can help me build a prototype.” The group exchanged determined nods, each of them now fully committed to bringing Nate’s idea to life. Amidst all the planning and the rapid-fire discussion of tasks, Kyle’s thoughts wandered momentarily to Autumn. He hadn’t seen her yet today, and as much as he enjoyed his friends' company, there was a restlessness tugging at him to catch up with her.

The next big item on their schedule was the practice football match against Alex's team, the first time they'd face off since the infamous incident that stirred up tension between Kyle and Alex. As the whistle blew to start the match, the atmosphere turned electric. Both sides pushed with everything they had, moving with an intensity that spoke of much more than just friendly competition. It was a high-stakes clash of skill and strategy. Each time Alex made a play, he'd glance at Kyle, a subtle smirk twisting his mouth, almost as if daring him. Kyle refused to back down, answering each challenge with his own.

By the end, both teams were exhausted, sweat dripping down their faces as they lined up to shake hands, the match resulting in a hard-fought draw. Kyle noticed Alex watching him with an expression that almost resembled respect.

Later that evening, as the sun began to set and the campus emptied out, Kyle and Autumn found each other in the usual place outside the art room. She looked a little weary from her singing practices, though her eyes sparkled with excitement as she described how her preparations were going. She was trying to learn every note, every intonation perfectly. Kyle listened, a smile tugging at his lips as he leaned against the wall.

"Sounds like you're really giving it your all, Autumn. I knew you would, though. You've always been determined like that." She laughed softly, tucking a stray strand of hair behind her ear. "Yeah, I guess I am. And you? Ready to make a masterpiece during the art program?" He shrugged playfully. "Oh, you know me. I just have to paint something that looks halfway decent, no big deal. I've got it covered."

They both laughed, sharing a familiar warmth that seemed to grow with each passing day. Just as they were about to part ways, Autumn's expression shifted to one of hesitation. She reached out and gently touched his hand, stopping him in his tracks. Kyle's pulse quickened, sensing something important was about to unfold.

"Kyle... there's something I need to tell you." Her voice was soft, and a hint of nervousness danced across her features.

His heart skipped a beat, and he tried to keep his voice steady. "Yeah? What is it?"

Autumn looked down, her fingers lightly tracing his hand as if to gather her thoughts. "I... well, I'd rather tell you on Sunday. Just before the fest. I hope that's okay." Kyle was taken aback but didn't press her further. He saw the seriousness in her eyes, the way she bit her lip, clearly deep in thought. The last thing he wanted was to make her uncomfortable or pressure her. So he simply nodded, his voice gentle. “Of course, Autumn. Whatever it is, I’ll be here to listen.” She seemed relieved, her shoulders relaxing as she flashed him a grateful smile. There was something intense, unspoken between them in that moment, as if they were both standing on the edge of something neither of them could quite name.

“Thank you, Kyle,” she whispered, squeezing his hand once before letting go. As she walked away, Kyle stood there, staring after her, his mind swirling with curiosity and anticipation. What could she possibly want to share with him?

After Kyle arrived home, his thoughts still lingered on Autumn’s cryptic words. He spent the entire ride wondering what she could possibly want to say to him on Sunday, turning over every conversation they’d had in the past few days to see if there was any clue he might have missed. He couldn’t shake the feeling that it was something important, something that would change things between them in ways he hadn’t even anticipated.

As he stepped through the front door, the warm scent of dinner greeted him. His mom, ever attentive, noticed his slightly distracted expression right away. “Kyle, you’ve been smiling since you got home,” she teased as she set the table. “Care to share what’s making you so happy?”

Kyle grinned, and for a moment, he hesitated. But then he decided to go for it. After all, his mom was the one person he trusted to understand. "Hey, Mom," he started as he took a seat at the dinner table, "there's this girl... Autumn."

The words felt strange but exciting to say out loud. His mom raised an eyebrow, her curiosity instantly piqued. "Oh, really?" she asked with a knowing smile. "So, tell me about her. Who is this Autumn?"

Kyle took a deep breath, gathering his thoughts. "She's... different, Mom. I don't even know how to put it into words," he began, a slight blush creeping up his cheeks. "She's kind, thoughtful, and just has this energy that makes you feel lighter around her. You know how some people just make the whole room feel warmer? She's like that." His mom watched him, an amused smile spreading across her face as he continued. "And she's got this way of seeing things... almost like she has her own unique perspective on everything. It's inspiring. And, well, I'm really lucky to have met her, I think."

His mom nodded, her smile widening. "This is the first time I've heard you talk about a girl like this, Kyle. She must be something special." Kyle chuckled, feeling a bit embarrassed but also happy to share this with her. "She really is. I don't know, she's just... she's made me see things differently, you know? She's a big part of why

I'm even excited about this cultural fest and all the projects. I feel like I'm trying harder, doing more, just because she believes in me."

As he spoke, his mom listened quietly, her warm smile never fading. When he finished, she rested a hand on his shoulder and said, "I'm happy you have someone like that in your life, Kyle. Sometimes, we meet people who bring out the best in us without even trying. It sounds like Autumn is that person for you."

"Yeah," he replied, a hint of a smile playing on his lips. "I think she is." They continued their dinner, and Kyle filled his mom in on the upcoming cultural fest events, mentioning the science project, the art class program, and, of course, the football match he and his friends were gearing up for. She listened patiently as he talked, occasionally nodding or asking a question, clearly enjoying this rare glimpse into his world.

"And so," he concluded, "Sunday's the day. That's when she said she'd tell me... well, whatever it is she wants to say." His mom gave him a reassuring smile. "It sounds like she has something special planned for you, Kyle. Whatever it is, I'm sure it'll be something worth remembering." Feeling lighter, Kyle helped his mom clear the dishes, still mulling over everything he had shared. Talking to his mom had somehow eased his restlessness, and now he felt a quiet excitement as he thought about Sunday. He was grateful for his mom's quiet support, knowing she wouldn't pry but would be there for him no matter what.

Later that night, Kyle lay in bed, his mind drifting between thoughts of Autumn and the upcoming events. He thought about the science project and Nate's excitement over it, the fierce rivalry with Alex's team that had fueled their last match, and the way Autumn had seemed so dedicated to her singing practice for the performance. She had been so immersed in her music, just as he was when he painted. There was something wonderful about seeing her work hard for something she was passionate about.

He turned over, smiling to himself as he imagined her reaction to each day of the fest. He could almost see her face light up during the art program, and he wondered what she'd think of the science project competition. Most of all, he thought about the words she'd whispered to him earlier that evening.

Whatever Autumn wanted to say on Sunday, Kyle felt ready to hear it. He drifted off to sleep, feeling content, knowing that whatever happened, he'd be there to listen. And in the back of his mind, he was already counting down the hours until he'd see her again.

The anticipation had been building in Kyle since he first set out for Autumn's house that morning. The promise of what she had to say, coupled with the plan he'd been forming to take her somewhere meaningful. As he revved his bike and left his house, Kyle couldn't shake the feeling that the day would bring something special. The bike's engine purred beneath him, though today it sounded a little different—maybe a bit deeper, more resonant, like the sound was matching the beat of his own thoughts. But he brushed it off, his mind too preoccupied with Autumn and their upcoming adventure.

He reached her driveway and there she was, standing in the morning sunlight, her hair catching the light in soft waves. She wore a warm smile, and as she stepped toward him, he felt that familiar feeling. It was as if every time he saw her, the world stilled just enough to let him take her in, every detail becoming vivid.

"You ready?" he asked with a grin, and she nodded.

Once she was seated comfortably behind him, Kyle pulled out of her driveway and headed toward the countryside. "I found a place I want to show you," he said over his shoulder. "It's supposed to be something special, but honestly, I've never seen it myself."

"Never seen it?" Autumn asked, leaning forward slightly, intrigued. "Are you taking me to some secret spot you've never been to?"

Kyle chuckled. "Maybe," he replied. "It's a place my dad used to talk about—a special tree on the edge of town. Apparently, it's one of the oldest orange trees here. The tree that inspired the town's name, he said. I've always wanted to see it."

As they rode, the scenery transformed into a golden mosaic of fallen leaves. The road became narrow, flanked by tall trees whose branches arched overhead, casting soft shadows on the path below. Leaves crunched beneath the tires as Kyle maneuvered the bike around gentle curves, and for a moment, it felt as though they were moving through a tunnel of trees, hidden from the rest of the world.

Autumn was silent, her arms wrapped around Kyle's waist, absorbing the scene with wide eyes. "This is beautiful," she murmured, and Kyle felt her shift slightly to look over his shoulder. The road looked like something out of a painting—softly golden, promising a new beginning, almost as if nature itself were inviting them to explore what lay ahead. They soon arrived at the spot his father had described, a secluded part of the woods where an ancient orange tree stood, its branches stretching wide with leaves that fluttered in the gentle breeze. Kyle parked the bike and turned to look at Autumn, her eyes reflecting the awe he felt. Without a word, they both climbed off the bike and walked toward the tree. "It's incredible," she whispered, her voice barely audible in the stillness. Kyle smiled, watching her as she took it all in. "My dad used to tell me that this tree has seen the town grow, seen countless seasons come and go," he said. "He always said it's a part of our roots, a symbol of the community and history we all share."

They moved closer to the tree, and Kyle gently touched its bark, feeling the rough texture under his fingertips. “It's strange,” he said. “Coming here makes me feel connected to him somehow. Like he's still a part of everything I do.”

Autumn stepped closer, her gaze warm and comforting. She didn’t say anything, but her presence was enough. Together, they wandered around the tree, the silence between them filled with unspoken understanding. The sun filtered through the branches, casting dappled shadows on the ground, and the soft rustle of leaves overhead created a calming soundtrack.

Eventually, Autumn spotted a small cluster of orange blossoms higher up in the branches. “It’s still blooming, even in the cooler season,” she said, smiling softly. “It feels like a hidden treasure.”
Kyle looked up, following her gaze, and nodded. “Maybe it’s a reminder,” he said thoughtfully. “A reminder that something beautiful can thrive even in unexpected times.” Autumn looked back at him, her eyes thoughtful, and after a brief pause, she asked, “Do you feel like this place lives up to what your dad told you?” Kyle considered her question, glancing back at the tree before answering. “Yeah, I think it does. And I’m glad I’m seeing it with you,” he added, his voice quiet but sincere. A soft blush colored Autumn’s cheeks, but she quickly looked away, pretending to focus on the ground. She took a step closer to the trunk, reaching out

to trace a name carved into the bark. "Do you think people come here to leave a mark?" she wondered aloud. "Maybe. Maybe they want to feel like they're a part of something bigger," Kyle replied, his gaze lingering on her as she inspected the tree with that curious look he'd come to admire. They spent a while just soaking in the tranquility of the place, exchanging small anecdotes about their families and dreams. Autumn opened up about her love for singing, how she sometimes felt nervous about performing even though she loved it. Kyle listened, feeling a renewed admiration for her passion and the way she threw herself into everything she loved.

A light breeze stirred the leaves, and Autumn closed her eyes, taking in a deep breath. "I feel like I could stay here forever," she said, her voice filled with contentment. Then she glanced back at Kyle. "Thank you for bringing me here, Kyle. I'll always remember this." He looked at her, a smile tugging at his lips. "I'm glad you like it." After a pause, he added, "It's just... nice, you know? Sharing something important with someone who understands." She held his gaze, her eyes soft. "Yeah. It really is." They stood there, side by side, as a peaceful silence settled over them. In that moment, surrounded by nature, Kyle felt as if everything in his life had led to this exact spot, this moment with her. And he couldn't shake the thought that this was where he was supposed to be.

They sat side by side beneath the sprawling branches of the ancient orange tree, its leaves casting intricate patterns of dappled sunlight across the ground. The air was thick with the earthy scent of fallen leaves and fresh soil, the gentle rustle of branches in the breeze adding a peaceful backdrop to their moment. For a few minutes, neither of them said anything, simply soaking in the quiet beauty around them. Kyle finally turned to her, his voice soft, "What's on your mind, Autumn?"

She hesitated, her gaze fixed on a spot in the distance. With a sigh, she rose to her feet, taking a few steps forward as if needing the space to confront her thoughts. "Do you... do you think the mistakes we make in the past eventually catch up with us?" Her voice was almost a whisper, laced with a vulnerability that caught Kyle off guard. Kyle blinked, a flicker of worry crossing his face. "Mistakes? Autumn, what are you talking about?"

She glanced back at him, a bitter smile on her lips. "I haven't told you everything, Kyle. I had friends before, people I thought would always be there. But... none of them are in my life anymore. Not because they chose to leave, but because I pushed them away." Her voice wavered as she looked down, her fingers nervously playing with the hem of her shirt. "I said things I shouldn't have. I hurt people I cared about... I don't even know why. I was so defensive, always pushing people away before they could get too close."

Kyle felt a pang in his chest at her words, wanting nothing more than to reach out and ease the pain he saw on her face. But he held back, letting her speak.

Autumn took a shaky breath, continuing, "I regret it every single day. I replay those moments in my mind, wondering if things could have been different if I had just... tried harder. If I'd been kinder." She wrapped her arms around herself, as though trying to hold herself together. "It hurts, Kyle. And I'm terrified that one day, all of that will come back to haunt me." He could see the raw regret etched on her face, the way her shoulders slumped as though carrying an invisible weight. He stood up, walking over to stand beside her. "Everyone deserves a second chance, Autumn," he said gently. "You've already repented for those mistakes, over and over. You don't need to keep punishing yourself."

She met his gaze, her eyes glistening with unshed tears. "But staying with me... it could hurt you too, Kyle. What if I mess this up too?" Her voice cracked as she looked away, her shoulders trembling. "You don't deserve that. I don't... I don't deserve you."

Kyle's chest tightened at her words, the pain in her eyes pulling at him like an undertow. He took a step closer, reaching out to gently lift her chin so she was looking at him. "Autumn," he murmured, his voice steady, "we've all made mistakes. And sometimes, yeah, those mistakes catch up with us. But that doesn't mean you don't deserve happiness, or love, or forgiveness. You're not defined by your past."

She looked at him, searching his face as if trying to find something that would disprove his words. A tear slipped down her cheek, and Kyle's thumb brushed it away, the touch gentle and warm. "I see the person you are now," he continued, his tone filled with quiet conviction. "And you're not the same as the person who made those mistakes. You've grown. You've changed. You've learned from them, haven't you?" Autumn nodded slowly, swallowing hard. "I have... but sometimes it feels like no matter how much I try to change; I can't escape what I did. I don't know if I'll ever be able to."

Kyle's hand lingered on her cheek for a moment, his heart pounding as he tried to find the right words. "Look, I don't expect you to be perfect. None of us are. But I want you to know that I'm here, with you, through all of it. I'll stand by you. And if you ever feel like you're slipping back, then lean on me." She closed her eyes, a soft, shuddering breath escaping her. "Why, Kyle? Why would you do that for me?"

"Because..." He hesitated, the words catching in his throat. A part of him wanted to confess everything right then and there, to tell her just how deeply he cared for her, how much he wanted to be the person she could rely on. But something held him back, a sense that this wasn't the moment for declarations. Instead, he settled for honesty. "Because you're worth it, Autumn. I see the good in you, the kindness, the strength. I don't care about your past. I just care about who you are now, here with me." A small smile tugged at her lips, though her eyes remained sad. "You make it sound so simple."

"It is, in a way," he replied, his voice soft but firm. "Life's complicated, but sometimes... sometimes the things that matter the most don't have to be." She gave a quiet laugh, wiping at her eyes. "You have a way of making me feel like maybe... just maybe, I'm not as terrible as I think I am."

"You're not," he said, his gaze unwavering. "You're one of the best people I know."

They stood in silence for a while, the weight of the conversation settling between them. Eventually, Autumn took a deep breath, her shoulders relaxing as though a weight had been lifted. She looked up at him, her expression softer, more at peace. "Thank you, Kyle," she murmured, her voice barely audible. "For... for everything."

He smiled, his heart swelling with a warmth he couldn't quite put into words. "Anytime," he replied, his voice gentle. As they returned to sit by the tree, the silence between them wasn't one of sadness or regret but of quiet understanding. The leaves rustled above, the sun dipping lower in the sky, casting a golden glow over the clearing. And in that moment, with the scent of earth and oranges in the air and Autumn by his side, Kyle knew he'd do anything to keep this feeling, this closeness, for as long as he could.

Kyle and Autumn walked side by side, the silence between them comfortable now, the weight of their conversation still hanging in the air. Kyle knew he had seen her most vulnerable in that moment, and for the first time, he felt like he truly understood the depth of the pain she carried. She wasn't just a strong girl who seemed to have everything together. There was so much more beneath the surface that she rarely let anyone see.

As they neared the spot where Kyle had parked his bike, Autumn's hand brushed against his. Hesitantly, she reached out and took his hand once again, this time not with the hesitance of someone who was unsure but with the quiet trust of someone who needed to feel anchored. Her fingers curled around his, delicate yet firm, as if she was afraid to let go. "Kyle..." she said quietly, her voice trembling ever so slightly. "I'm not a burden to you, am I?" The question was simple but laced with a vulnerability Kyle had never heard in her voice before. "I just hope I don't hurt you," she added, her words carrying the weight of a deep fear, one that was etched into her heart from the mistakes she had made in the past.

Kyle stopped in his tracks, his gaze softening as he turned to face her. He could see the uncertainty in her eyes, the way she sought reassurance like a child who was afraid of being abandoned. The image hit him with the force of a tidal wave—Autumn, this seemingly perfect, untouchable girl, holding so much fear of being too much for others. He placed both his hands on her shoulders, pulling her closer with an intensity that spoke of his desire to protect her, to make sure she knew that she wasn't alone.

"Autumn," he said, his voice calm but firm, "even if you stabbed me, I'd just apologize to you for getting my blood on your clothes."

The words seemed to resonate between them, full of meaning that she hadn't expected. Autumn's eyes widened, her breath catching in her throat. A single tear rolled down her cheek, and before she could even think about stopping herself, she wrapped her arms around Kyle, pulling him into a tight hug. She needed him, needed the warmth of his presence, the quiet reassurance he offered so freely. Kyle's arms instinctively wrapped around her, holding her close. He didn't mind the way her tears stained his shirt or the way she clung to him, as if she was afraid he might slip away. He patted her head gently, offering her comfort in the only way he knew how.

"You're not a burden," he murmured softly, the words a promise, an affirmation. "I'm here for you. You never have to worry about hurting me. Not now, not ever." They stood there for a while, wrapped in each other's arms, the world around them fading into the background. The weight of her worries and fears seemed to melt away with each passing moment, and for the first time, Autumn felt like she could breathe again. She pulled back slightly, her tear-streaked face lifting to meet his gaze.

"How do I even thank you?" she asked, her voice barely above a whisper. There was so much she wanted to say, but the words felt inadequate, as though nothing could truly express what she was feeling in that moment.

Kyle smiled softly, brushing a stray lock of hair from her face. "You don't need to thank me," he replied, his voice gentle but resolute. "I'm just doing what any person who cares about you would do. You're not alone, Autumn."

She looked at him, her heart full, a warmth spreading through her chest. There was so much she wanted to say, but somehow, just being there, in that moment, was enough. She nodded, her lips trembling slightly as she fought back another wave of emotion. Together, they walked the rest of the way to the bike. Kyle helped Autumn onto it before mounting it himself, the familiar rumble of the engine grounding them both in the moment. He didn't want to think about the future, about what would come next, because right now, everything felt perfect—just the two of them, together, in this fleeting moment of peace.

As they started the engine and headed down the winding road, Kyle felt a strange sense of contentment. He wasn't sure what the future held, but he knew one thing for certain: no matter what, he would be there for Autumn. She had been through so much, and he wasn't about to let her face any of it alone. Autumn clung to him as they rode, her arms wrapped around his waist, her head resting against his back. It was as if they were suspended in time, the world moving around them but not touching them, not intruding on the quiet connection they shared. The wind rushed past them, the sound of the engine roaring in their ears, but all Kyle could hear was the steady beat of his heart and the gentle rhythm of Autumn's breathing against his back. The road ahead was uncertain, but for now, he didn't care. He had her by his side, and that was all that mattered.

As they rode down the winding road, the air cooled around them, signaling that dusk was approaching. The sun dipped lower in the sky, casting long shadows from the trees that lined the road, and a soft orange glow wrapped around everything, making it feel like the world was holding its breath. The quiet companionship he shared with Autumn on these rides made everything feel calm, even as they drifted into evening. “It’s getting pretty late,” Kyle said over the sound of the engine, glancing back at her as they passed beneath the rustling branches overhead. “I should probably drop you home quickly so you’re not out too late.”

Autumn’s hand tightened slightly around his waist, and she seemed to be mulling over something. She nodded, leaning a little closer to him so she wouldn’t have to shout. “Yeah, I guess so,” she said, her voice soft and thoughtful, almost as if she were savoring the last few moments of their time together for the day. After a moment, she added, “So...are you all set for tomorrow? With the art showcase, I mean?” Kyle blinked, her words pulling him back to reality. Tomorrow’s showcase had completely slipped his mind in the excitement of today. He laughed a little, rubbing the back of his neck. “Actually...no,” he admitted, chuckling. “I still need to pick up some art supplies. I forgot I was running low.” Autumn’s laugh joined his, though he could see the small furrow of concern that formed between her brows. “Kyle, it’s already getting dark,” she said, her voice light but carrying a hint of worry. “If you drop me home and then go out for shopping, you’ll hardly have any time left for yourself tonight.” Kyle shrugged, smiling as though it were nothing. “Eh, I’ll manage. I mean, I’ve pulled all-nighters before. A little last-minute shopping is no big deal.”

But Autumn wasn't so easily convinced. She studied him with a critical eye, a gentle yet firm look that showed she was already forming a better plan. "How about this," she suggested, tapping his shoulder lightly. "You can drop me off near the bus stop instead. It's closer for you, and I'll be just fine from there. That way, you won't have to worry about time as much." Kyle hesitated, glancing back at her with a raised brow. "Autumn...are you sure? I don't mind taking you all the way. You know that."

She laughed softly, patting his shoulder as if to ease his concern. "Kyle, you've already done so much for me today. I don't want to make things harder for you when you've got your own plans. Besides," she added, tilting her head with a smile, "I like that you care enough to worry, but I think I'll be okay." Kyle sighed, nodding. He knew there was no arguing with her once she'd made up her mind. "Alright, alright," he agreed at last, relenting with a small smile. "But only if you promise to text me as soon as you're home, okay?" Autumn's eyes sparkled, and she lifted her hand in a playful salute. "Yes, sir. You have my word."

They continued on the road together, the landscape gradually shifting as they approached town. The trees were now lined with hints of red and orange, and leaves covered the ground in patches, signaling the slow but steady arrival of autumn. Kyle couldn't help but glance back every so often, catching glimpses of Autumn's face in the golden hour light. The sight of her in the fading day felt almost dreamlike, and he wished, just for a moment, that time would slow down. Suddenly, the sound of a siren broke through the peaceful quiet of the road. Kyle turned his head, seeing flashing lights approaching from behind. He guided the bike carefully to the side, giving way to an ambulance that sped past, its lights cutting through the dimming light. Kyle felt Autumn's arms tighten slightly around his waist, and when he glanced back, he noticed her eyes were closed, her lips moving as if in a silent prayer.

He smiled to himself, touched by her gesture. When the ambulance was out of sight, he said quietly, "You're too pure, Autumn." She looked up, meeting his gaze with a soft expression. "It's just... you never know what people in that ambulance might be going through," she replied, her voice carrying a gentle understanding. "The least we can do is send them a bit of hope. Even if we don't know them, a prayer never goes to waste." Kyle nodded, feeling warmth bloom in his chest. For all the worries she had shared with him recently, Autumn's heart seemed to remain open to others, to the world, in a way that only deepened his admiration for her. The silence that followed was peaceful, and they didn't need words to fill it. The steady hum of the bike and the whisper of the evening breeze were enough.

They soon approached the bus stop, the street lamps flickering on one by one, casting warm yellow circles of light onto the pavement. The stop was empty, save for a stray cat curled up on one of the benches. Kyle pulled up slowly, guiding the bike to a careful stop just beside the shelter. He parked, letting the engine die down as the sounds of the evening settled around them. The night air was crisp, a gentle breeze rustling through the trees that lined the street. Kyle's motorcycle idled in front of the bus stop, the engine's hum a soft contrast to the stillness around them. Kyle glanced at Autumn, who had her arms folded in front of her, sitting on the bench at the bus stop. She was staring off into the distance, the faint glow of the streetlamp casting a soft light on her face. "I'll stay until you get on the bus," Kyle said, his voice firm yet gentle. He wasn't going anywhere until he knew she was safe.

Autumn had already tried to convince him otherwise, saying that he didn't need to wait with her, but he was insistent. He wouldn't leave her until she was on her way. The worry in his eyes was hard for Autumn to ignore. She looked at him, realizing how much he cared, and with a sigh, she resigned herself to the fact that he wasn't going to leave. "I told you, I'll be fine," she said, a playful tone creeping into her voice. But even as she said the words, she appreciated the gesture. She couldn't remember the last time someone had cared so much about her well-being.

"Yeah, well, I'd feel better knowing you were safe," Kyle replied, giving her a soft smile before taking a seat beside her on the bench. For a moment, they just sat in silence, the quiet comfort of each other's company filling the space between them. "So, ready for tomorrow?" Autumn asked, breaking the silence. Her voice was filled with curiosity, and there was a spark of excitement in her eyes. The festival, the competition, the football match—it was all so close now. Kyle could sense the nervous energy building in her, and he felt it too. Tomorrow would be a big day for both of them.

"Yeah, I think so," Kyle replied, stretching his legs out in front of him. "I'm just hoping we don't mess up anything in the project. You know how Sam gets when things don't go as planned." Autumn chuckled at the thought. "Sam is always like that," she said, shaking her head. "But you guys will do fine. You always manage to pull things off." Kyle smiled, grateful for her words of encouragement. They had spent so much time working on the project, and even though he wasn't entirely sure of the outcome, he knew they had given it their best effort. And with Autumn by his side, he felt like they could conquer anything. As they continued talking about their preparations, a distant sound broke through the conversation—soft at first, then growing louder. Kyle turned to see a small child walking towards them with his mother. The child was crying, his tiny hands clutching tightly onto his mother's fingers as he tugged at her.

"He's sad that I won't give him sweets," the mother said with a smile, her voice warm and patient. "He's been asking me all day." Autumn and Kyle both laughed softly at the sight, and Autumn couldn't help but feel a sense of sympathy for the little boy. He was so small, so innocent, his world still so new and full of emotions that he didn't yet understand how to express. Without thinking, Autumn stood up from the bench and walked toward the child. The boy's tear-streaked face looked up at her as she knelt down in front of him. She gently pinched his chubby cheeks, making a silly face to make him laugh. Her voice was soft, sweet, and reassuring as she spoke.

"Hey there, little one," Autumn said, her smile wide and warm. "If you stop crying, I'll give you a candy. Deal?" The boy's eyes widened at the mention of candy, and his tears stopped almost instantly. His tiny hands released his mother's fingers, and he looked at Autumn with wide, hopeful eyes. "Really?" he asked, his voice small and uncertain.

"Really," Autumn confirmed with a nod. "But you've got to promise to be a good boy and stop crying, okay?" The boy hesitated for a moment, then nodded, his face breaking into a shy but genuine smile. "Okay."

Autumn reached into her pocket and pulled out a small candy, holding it out to the boy. He took it eagerly, his face lighting up with joy as he clutched the candy in his hand. Autumn smiled, watching as the boy's tears had disappeared completely. Kyle stood quietly behind Autumn, observing her with a soft smile. He couldn't help but marvel at the way she interacted with the child, how easily she calmed him down with just a few simple words. There was something about the way she spoke to him, the way she made him feel safe and understood, that touched Kyle deeply. He felt his chest tighten as he watched her, realizing just how much he admired her.

In that moment, he thought to himself, There are poets in this world, but you, Autumn, you yourself are poetry. The way she moved, the way she spoke, the way she made the world seem kinder—there was something magical about her that left him in awe. He knew, deep down, that he wanted her by his side forever. The boy waved goodbye to Autumn, his smile still wide as he clutched the candy in his hand. Autumn stood up, turning back toward Kyle with a playful grin on her face.

"See? I told you it would work," she said, her eyes sparkling with mischief. Kyle couldn't help but smile in return. "You're amazing with kids," he said, his voice soft with admiration. "I've never seen anyone calm someone down like that before." Autumn laughed, brushing her hair back from her face. "It's easy when you know how to talk to them," she said. "I guess I've had a lot of practice."

Kyle looked at her for a moment, his heart swelling with affection. "I think you'd be great with a family someday," he said, his voice almost a whisper. Autumn's eyes widened slightly, and she glanced at him in surprise. "A family?" she repeated, her voice soft. "You really think that?" Kyle's heart skipped a beat as he realized what he'd just said. He had spoken from the heart without thinking, and now he couldn't take the words back. But instead of feeling embarrassed, he felt a sense of peace. It felt right. She felt right. "Yeah," he said, his voice steady and confident. "I do."

The bus pulled up at that moment, and Autumn glanced at it before looking back at Kyle. "Well, I guess this is it," she said, her tone light but there was a softness in her eyes that he could see. "I'll see you tomorrow." Kyle smiled, nodding. "See you tomorrow, Autumn."

As she boarded the bus, she turned and waved at him one last time. Kyle stood there, watching her as the bus slowly pulled away. A gentle smile lingered on his lips as he realized just how much she meant to him. He knew that whatever the future held, he wanted her in it.

The night had fallen quietly around him, the stars now beginning to shimmer in the sky as Kyle sat on the bench by the bus stop. His hands rested on his knees, his eyes fixed on the street where Autumn's bus had disappeared into the night. His heart was full, a warmth settling deep within him that he couldn't shake. He had never felt like this before—so sure, so at peace with everything.

Today had been perfect. From the moment he had met Autumn, to the way she had smiled, to the way they had talked so freely with one another. To see her laughing, so carefree, to watch her comfort that little boy—it was a side of her that Kyle was beginning to see more of, and it made his heart swell. She was so much more than just the girl who sat next to him in art class. She was kind, gentle, and so incredibly strong, even if she didn't always see it in herself.

Kyle sat there for what seemed like an eternity, just taking everything in. The crisp air, the distant hum of the town, the lingering echo of their conversation. It felt like everything had clicked into place. He hadn't expected to feel so much, so fast, but there it was. The moment he realized that maybe he didn't need to search for something more—because he had found it, right in front of him. The sound of a motorcycle engine in the distance brought him out of his thoughts. He shook his head, chuckling softly to himself. "I better get going before it gets too late," he muttered to no one in particular. He knew he had to pick up the supplies for the festival, and now that he'd had his time to reflect, it was time to get to work.

Kyle stood up, dusting off his jeans, and walked over to his bike. As he revved the engine, the familiar roar of the motor calmed his nerves. He was used to this feeling—the wind in his hair, the streets ahead of him. But tonight, it felt different. There was a sense of purpose to the ride, a sense of clarity that he hadn't had before.

The ride to the supply store was short, and Kyle quickly parked his bike near the entrance. He walked inside, the soft hum of the store's fluorescent lights above him. The aisles were stocked with everything he needed for the festival—paintbrushes, canvases, sketchpads, and more. Kyle picked out his supplies with ease, the act almost second nature to him now. He had been painting for years, but this time felt different. It wasn't just about the project. It wasn't just about the competition. It was about the experience—the opportunity to share something of himself with those around him, and to have Autumn there, cheering him on.

As he walked through the aisles, he remembered his mom's request for snacks. She had been so supportive of him, and he was grateful for that. He grabbed a few bags of her favorite snacks, then headed to the checkout. The store was empty save for a few customers, the cashier ringing him up without much conversation. It was late, and Kyle was ready to get home, but he couldn't help but feel a little more energized than usual.

When he finished, he quickly grabbed the bags and walked out to his bike, a sense of satisfaction building in his chest. The night was still young, but he knew his mom would be waiting for him, and he couldn't wait to tell her about his day. He smiled to himself, thinking of how happy she would be. She'd always been the one to encourage him, to remind him to take time for himself, and to focus on the things that mattered.

As Kyle rode home, his thoughts once again drifted to Autumn. It was like she belonged in his life. He felt lucky to have met her. And for the first time in a long time, he realized that maybe it wasn't just about getting through the days—it was about finding joy in them, about finding the beauty in the simple moments, the ones that made everything feel perfect. Halfway through his ride, as he neared the intersection near his neighborhood, Kyle heard the unmistakable sound of sirens approaching. He glanced over his shoulder and saw the flashing lights of an ambulance drawing near. His heart skipped a beat. The sound of the sirens seemed to echo in the still night, and Kyle instinctively slowed his bike down, pulling to the side of the road.

He didn't know why, but as the ambulance passed by, he felt a strange sense of solidarity. Without thinking, he bowed his head and offered a quick prayer. It was a simple gesture, a wish for the people inside the ambulance to be okay, to find peace, to find hope. He didn't know who they were, didn't know what they were going through, but in that moment, he felt connected to them.

He let out a breath as the ambulance disappeared into the distance, the lights fading in the rearview mirror. Then, he laughed softly to himself. "She really has influenced me, huh?" Kyle said, the realization making him chuckle. He was surprised by how natural it had felt, how instinctual the prayer had been. Autumn's words, the way she spoke about sending prayers to those who needed them—it had stuck with him. Maybe it was her pure heart, or maybe it was the way she saw the world, but Kyle found himself changed, in a way he wasn't entirely sure he understood. But it felt good. It felt right.

With that, he turned the bike back onto the road and continued his ride home, his thoughts no longer clouded with uncertainty. When Kyle finally reached home, he parked the bike in the driveway, grabbed the snacks for his mom, and headed inside. The house was quiet, but he could hear the soft hum of the television from the living room. His mom was sitting on the couch, sipping a cup of tea. She looked up when she heard him enter, her face lighting up with a smile. "Hey, how was your day?" she asked, her voice warm with concern.

Kyle smiled back, handing her the snacks. "It was great. I've got all my supplies ready for tomorrow. I'll be up late tonight, but it's all coming together. Oh, and I've got something to tell you about Autumn." His mom raised an eyebrow, intrigued. Kyle sat down beside her and began recounting his day—how he and Autumn had spent the afternoon together, the way she had interacted with the child at the bus stop, how kind and beautiful she was. His mom listened intently, her smile never fading.

"That sounds wonderful," she said when he was done. "I'm so glad to hear that. You deserve to be happy."

Kyle nodded, his heart swelling. "Yeah, I think I am," he said quietly.

He thanked his mom for dinner, then headed upstairs to his room. He laid out all of his painting supplies on the desk, making sure everything was ready for the morning. The festival was almost here, and Kyle felt the excitement building again. He set an alarm for early morning and, with a contented sigh, climbed into bed. Kyle drifted off to sleep with a smile on his face, knowing that tomorrow would be another step in the journey he never expected to take—but one he was glad to be on.

Kyle's body finally gave in to exhaustion after the long, eventful day. The world around him was a hazy blur as he drifted into a heavy, much-needed sleep, thoughts of Autumn still dancing in his mind. Her laughter, her smile, the way she gently held his hand and reassured him with her words. Everything seemed surreal. His last conscious thought was a sense of deep contentment, an unfamiliar yet comforting feeling, as he finally let himself fall into peaceful slumber. But peace was fleeting. A voice called out, sharp and insistent, shattering his dreams. "Kyle!"

He stirred, trying to hold onto sleep, but the voice persisted, pulling him out of his drowsy haze. Blinking, he squinted into the darkness, struggling to separate dreams from reality. The voice grew clearer. His mom was calling him from downstairs. Why would she be waking him up at this hour? "What is it, Mom?" he asked, his voice thick with sleep as he rose, rubbing his eyes. The room was dimly lit by the soft glow from the hallway, casting long shadows across his bed and walls. An odd sense of foreboding crept into him as he got up, the back of his mind sensing something wrong even before his mom spoke. "There's a call for you, Kyle," she said quietly. There was an unusual quality to her tone, one that made his pulse quicken.

"A call?" he echoed, his mind still foggy. He couldn't remember the last time he'd gotten a call at this hour. It wasn't like his friends to call him late at night, and his mind raced, trying to think of who it could be. As he walked downstairs, the air around him felt thick and heavy, pressing down on his chest. His mom stood by the phone, clutching it as if it were something fragile. Her expression was calm but strangely tense, a subtle tightness around her eyes that Kyle hadn't seen before. She looked at him with an unreadable expression as he approached.

"Kyle, someone's asking for you," she murmured

Kyle's heart pounded faster as he reached out for the receiver, feeling the weight of the phone in his hand. He lifted it to his ear, his mind running wild with possibilities. "Hello?" The line crackled slightly before a soft, unsteady voice spoke up. "Is this Kyle?" The voice was faint, barely audible, and filled with a trembling hesitance. "Yeah...this is Kyle. Who's calling?" His heartbeat thundered in his ears; each beat louder than the last as he tried to identify the voice on the other end. He sensed something off—something that made the hairs on the back of his neck stand up. It was as if a shadow had fallen over his world, an ominous feeling he couldn't shake. "I'm a friend of Autumn," the voice replied, faltering, as if each word was a struggle. "Autumn...she's in the hospital."

Kyle's world stopped. The words echoed in his mind, repeating over and over until they didn't sound like words anymore. Hospital? Autumn? It couldn't be right. He must've heard wrong. "What?" he choked out. His fingers tightened around the receiver, gripping it so hard his knuckles turned white. "What happened to Autumn?"

There was a long pause on the other end, filled with nothing but the sound of shallow, shaky breaths. Finally, the voice spoke again, this time even quieter. "She was in an accident...right after she got off the bus. I thought...you should know." The world spun around him, colors fading, sounds dulling. Everything felt unreal, like he was trapped in some twisted nightmare. This couldn't be happening. Not to Autumn. She had been perfectly fine just hours ago, laughing and talking, full of life. He refused to believe it. "No, that can't be...she was fine. She was just fine!" His voice broke, desperation lacing every word. "Are you sure?" he asked, even though he knew it was a foolish question. The sinking feeling in his stomach told him it was true, that his worst fear had somehow come to life.

The voice on the other end cracked with emotion. "I'm so sorry, Kyle. I...I thought you should be there. She's...she's not well. Please come if you can." Kyle didn't remember dropping the phone, but suddenly it was on the floor, the dial tone buzzing hollowly from the receiver. His mother stepped forward, her hand on his shoulder, worry etched across her face. "Kyle? What's wrong?"

"Autumn is in the hospital," he whispered, the words tasting bitter on his tongue. "She was in an accident..." The sentence hung in the air, cold and cruel, as if saying it aloud would make it more real. He felt like he was floating, disconnected from his own body as the reality of the situation settled over him like a dark cloud. His mother's face softened with shock and sympathy. "Oh, Kyle..." She tried to pull him into a hug, but he pulled away, his mind already miles away. He couldn't stand still, couldn't bear to be here. He needed to be with her.

"I have to go," he said, his voice unsteady. "I have to see her." He turned and rushed toward the door, barely hearing his mom's words as she called after him. His mind was racing, his thoughts a jumbled mess of fear and dread. He couldn't lose her. Not after everything. He grabbed his keys, fumbling with them as he ran to his bike. His hands shook so badly it took him three tries to get the key in the ignition. His chest felt tight, his breaths coming in short, ragged gasps as he started the engine. The roar of the bike was almost comforting, grounding him in the present, if only for a moment.
He sped down the street, the cool night air hitting his face as he rode, each second feeling like an eternity. The world around him was a blur of lights and shadows, but he didn't care. Nothing mattered except getting to her. The streets seemed empty, almost surreal in their stillness, as if the whole world had gone silent in sympathy.

As he approached a red light, he slowed down, barely aware of his surroundings. His mind was consumed by thoughts of Autumn—her face, her voice, the way she laughed. He couldn't shake the image of her lying in a hospital bed, hurt and alone. The thought made his chest ache, a dull, unbearable pain that seemed to seep into his very soul. "Autumn, please be okay," he whispered, his voice barely audible above the hum of the engine. Finally, he reached the hospital. The stark white building loomed ahead of him, cold and unwelcoming under the harsh fluorescent lights. He parked his bike haphazardly, not caring if it was in a designated spot or not. All he could think about was getting to her. He ran inside, his shoes squeaking on the polished floors as he made his way to the front desk. The nurse looked up, startled, as he approached. "Can I help you?" she asked, her tone professional but slightly wary.

"I'm here for Autumn... she was in an accident," he said, his voice trembling. "I need to see her."
The nurse's face softened slightly as she typed something into the computer. "She was admitted just a little while ago. Room 314, down the hall on your left."
Without waiting for a thank you, Kyle turned and rushed down the hallway, his heart pounding harder with each step. The hallway seemed endless, stretching out before him like a dark tunnel, each step echoing in the silence. He could barely breathe, his chest tight with anxiety.

Kyle's heart pounded in his chest as he neared Room 314. The hallway felt longer than ever, each step bringing him closer to an unbearable reality. The dull, sterile lights above flickered as if they, too, were unsure of what was about to unfold. His hands trembled, his legs barely carrying him, and his breath came in shallow gasps. His mind was reeling with a whirlwind of thoughts: Autumn's fine, she's going to be fine. It's just an accident. She's strong. She'll pull through. But nothing seemed certain anymore.

As he reached the door, he saw them—two figures standing outside, their faces a reflection of everything he feared. The weight of the world seemed to press down on him with each step. He recognized them instantly: Autumn's parents. Her mom was crying, her hands pressed to her face as her dad stood beside her, his posture tense and helpless as he tried to console her. The sight of Autumn's mom—someone who had always been so kind and welcoming—broken and shaking, shattered Kyle's resolve.

He stopped a few feet away from them, his throat tight with emotion. He wanted to speak, to offer comfort, but the words wouldn't come. There was nothing to say that could undo what had happened, nothing that would make this better. Her dad looked up at him, his face softening as he recognized Kyle. "You must be Kyle," he said, extending his hand. Kyle could barely see through the fog of his own tears, but he reached out shakily, taking the offered hand with a firm shake. "Yeah... I'm Kyle," he said, his voice hoarse, barely above a whisper.

Her mom's gaze shifted from her husband to Kyle, and her sobs grew louder. "Look what happened to her..." she cried, her words piercing through Kyle's heart like a knife. She reached out, grasping his hand, her grip tight and desperate. "She's just a girl... She didn't deserve this..."
Kyle felt a lump form in his throat, and tears he had been trying to hold back since the call broke free, streaming down his face. He wiped them away furiously, his hands shaking. He had to stay strong. He couldn't fall apart, not now. Not when Autumn needed him most.

"How long has she been inside?" Kyle asked, his voice trembling. Her dad glanced at the clock on the wall before answering. "About twenty minutes now," he said quietly, the words seeming to carry an unspeakable weight. Kyle nodded, his mind racing. Twenty minutes. That wasn't a lot of time. That didn't mean the worst was happening. But everything inside him screamed that this was it—that this could be the moment when everything changed. "I should have been there for her," he thought bitterly. I should have insisted more. I should have just taken her home myself.

Her dad seemed to read his mind. "She's stubborn, just like her mother," he said with a half-hearted smile, though his eyes were full of worry. "She didn't want to trouble anyone. She insisted she was fine." Kyle felt a wave of guilt crash over him. He had insisted too, but she wouldn't listen. Autumn had always been so determined, so independent, never wanting to burden anyone, and now—now she was paying the price for it. The thought gnawed at him like a constant ache, and he swallowed it down with difficulty. He had to be there for her. She needed him.

Kyle drew a shaky breath, steadying himself as much as he could. He reached for his phone, dialing Sam's number. Sam picked up almost instantly, the usual humor in his voice replaced by worry when he heard Kyle's tone. "Sam... something happened," Kyle managed, his voice barely holding together. "Autumn—she... she's been in an accident. She's in the hospital." There was a beat of silence before Sam's voice came back, all traces of levity gone. "We're coming, Kyle. Hang in there."

Within minutes, Sam, Nate, Ryder and Ryan arrived at the hospital, each of them looking as shaken as Kyle felt. They gathered around him, forming a protective circle, each taking turns offering words of comfort and solidarity. For once, Sam was speechless. Ryan placed a hand on Kyle's shoulder, his steady presence grounding him. "Man, she's strong. She's going to pull through," Ryan said, his voice soft but resolute. The words were reassuring, though Kyle could see the fear etched into each of their faces.

Autumn's mom looked at Kyle's friends, offering them a tearful, grateful nod. "Thank you all for coming," she said softly. "It means so much... she's lucky to have friends like you." "Anything for her," Nate said, his usual calm composure strained. "We'll stay as long as it takes."

The hours felt like an eternity. Kyle and his friends kept vigil outside the room, each passing minute increasing the weight of uncertainty. The hospital's white walls and antiseptic smell were suffocating, and Kyle kept pacing, his thoughts spiraling in circles as he tried to brace himself for whatever news might come. The memories of the day played over and over in his mind, like a reel stuck on loop. Autumn's laughter, her smile, the way she'd gently held his hand— all of it felt unbearably fragile now.

As Kyle stood with his friends just outside Autumn's room, the weight of everything began pressing down on him. He tried to collect his thoughts, but his mind was a storm, each wave of emotion hitting harder than the last. His friends watched him closely, each of them unsure how to console him in a situation that was beyond any of their experiences. Kyle took a few steps away from Autumn's parents, his friends trailing along in silence. He pulled out his phone and dialed his mom. His voice was barely a whisper when she picked up. "Mom... can you come to the hospital?" he asked, barely able to hold back his emotions.

Without a second thought, his mom replied, "I'm already on my way, Kyle." Kyle ended the call and stuffed his phone back into his pocket, staring at the ground. He rubbed his hands over his face, trying to compose himself, but the pain was just too raw. He could feel his friends' supportive presence around him, but he couldn't bring himself to look at them.

After a moment, he broke the silence, his voice trembling. "You know, when everything finally feels like it's falling into place... God just decides to throw an axe, tearing it all apart." His friends exchanged uncertain glances, taken aback by the bitterness in his voice. They'd never heard Kyle sound so defeated, so utterly vulnerable. Ryder reached out, placing a reassuring hand on Kyle's shoulder. "Stay strong, man," he said gently, trying to offer some comfort. "We're all here with you."

Ryan added softly, "God has mysterious ways of working, Kyle. Sometimes we can't see the reason right away, but maybe there's a bigger picture we're not seeing yet." Kyle shook his head, a hint of frustration creeping into his expression. He looked at each of them, his eyes filled with pain and disbelief. "But... Autumn is all I ever wanted," he choked out. "She's the only one who gave my life meaning, something I could actually strive toward. And just when things start to make sense, God... he just takes it all away. Why? What did I do wrong?"

Ryan, Ryder, and Nate fell silent, unable to find words that could ease the ache Kyle was feeling. Sam, ever the jokester and usually the most confident, simply placed a comforting hand on Kyle's shoulder, patting him gently as he tried to think of what to say. "Come on, Kyle," Sam said quietly, attempting to keep his tone calm. "We still don't know how serious things are. She's in good hands. For all we know, she could be okay. Maybe she got lucky."

Nate nodded, stepping forward and meeting Kyle's gaze. "She's strong, Kyle. We all know she is. And she'd want you to believe in her." But despite their words, Kyle couldn't stop the silent tears that began trailing down his cheeks. He knew his friends were trying their best, but nothing they could say would ease the suffocating weight in his chest.

Just then, his mom arrived, rushing through the hallway toward them. She spotted Kyle and immediately opened her arms, pulling him into a tight embrace. She held him close, rubbing his back gently as he buried his face in her shoulder, letting out the tears he'd been holding back. It was rare for Kyle to be this vulnerable, even in front of his mom, but the overwhelming fear and pain left him no choice. She whispered softly, "I'm here, Kyle. It's going to be okay." After a moment, she pulled back, brushing his hair from his forehead and looking him over with concerned eyes. "Where are Autumn's parents?"

Sam stepped forward and pointed them out at the end of the hallway, where they were seated in silent vigil, her mother still dabbing her eyes with a tissue. Kyle's mom nodded, giving Kyle one last squeeze before heading over to offer whatever comfort she could to Autumn's parents. Kyle wiped his face, taking a steadying breath, and then turned back to his friends. He forced a weak smile, trying to gather himself.

"You guys should probably head home," he said softly, his voice barely above a whisper. "I'm not... I'm not going to be able to make it tomorrow or the day after. There's no way I could focus on the fest like this." But Sam wasn't having it. He shook his head, crossing his arms defiantly. "Shut up, Kyle. We're not leaving you alone here." Kyle attempted a small laugh, but it came out as more of a sigh. "Look, Autumn wouldn't want you guys missing out on the fest because of her. She'd be mad if she knew I was keeping you here instead of letting you go and have fun." He tried to convince them, explaining how much effort they'd all put into preparing for the festival. "You've all been working so hard for this," he insisted. "Autumn would hate to know that I'm making you skip it. Go, enjoy it... for her."

There was a long, tense pause as his friends looked at one another, hesitant to leave him in such a vulnerable state. Finally, Nate spoke up, his voice soft but resolute.

"Kyle, we're here for you, no matter what. But... if it's what you really want, we'll go. Just know we're only a call away. If you need us, we'll come back in a heartbeat."

Ryan nodded in agreement, squeezing Kyle's shoulder in a reassuring gesture. "You've got us, Kyle. We'll check in with you every hour, and we'll be back the second you need us." Kyle smiled, feeling grateful for their understanding. "Thanks, guys. Really."

With one last round of goodbyes and supportive pats on the back, his friends slowly began to leave, each of them casting one last look at Kyle, silently promising to be there if he needed them. As they disappeared down the hallway, Kyle felt the loneliness creeping in, but he also knew they'd done what he'd asked because they cared deeply for him—and because they trusted him to handle this his own way. He took another deep breath, trying to steady himself as he sat back down outside Autumn's room. His mom returned shortly after, placing a gentle hand on his shoulder as they waited together in quiet anticipation. It was going to be a long night, but with his mother's comforting presence beside him, Kyle felt a small glimmer of strength return. He wouldn't leave Autumn's side, no matter what.

As Kyle and his mom sat quietly with Autumn's parents in the waiting area, an almost unbearable tension filled the air. The stark hospital walls seemed to close in around them, amplifying every whispered conversation, every distant beep of medical machines. Each of them was locked in their own thoughts, holding onto any scrap of hope they could find. Kyle, though usually confident and grounded, found himself struggling to stay calm. He stole glances at Autumn's parents, her mom visibly trembling, clinging to her husband's arm. It felt as though the world had shattered around them, leaving only the unknown as they waited.

Then, the doors of the operating room opened with a soft creak. A nurse emerged, her expression calm yet serious, and she walked over to them. Kyle could feel his pulse racing; he braced himself as she approached, his stomach knotted in fear. Autumn's parents immediately rose to their feet, their expressions hopeful yet apprehensive. The nurse took a slow, deep breath and addressed them with a gentle tone. "The doctors have managed to stabilize Autumn," she began. Her words seemed to lift a huge burden off of everyone's shoulders. Kyle exhaled in relief, feeling his muscles relax just a bit. Her mother covered her mouth with her hands, the faintest glimmer of hope brightening her tear-streaked face. "But..." The nurse's voice wavered slightly, and the relief that had started to fill the room faded. "There's some damage to her head from the accident. She's going to need time to heal, and the doctor would like to speak with you about the specifics tomorrow morning. For tonight, all we can do is let her rest and keep her stable."

Kyle could barely process the nurse's words, but he knew this was better news than he had dared to hope for. He glanced at Autumn's parents, seeing the bittersweet mix of relief and anxiety on their faces. Kyle knew he had to be strong, not only for himself but also for Autumn's family. They all deserved someone to lean on right now.

Turning to his mom, Kyle said softly, "Maybe you could take Mrs. Smith home for the night so she can get some rest? I'll stay here with Mr. Smith and keep him company." Kyle's mom nodded in agreement, and, sensing that Mrs. Smith could use some encouragement, she gently took her hand.

Mrs. Smith looked uncertain but exhausted, the day's events clearly weighing on her. She hesitated, glancing at her husband, who gently encouraged her, "Honey, you should head home and get some rest. We'll need all the strength we can get tomorrow." After a moment, she agreed, and Kyle's mom put an arm around her shoulders, guiding her toward the exit. "Call me if you need anything, Kyle," his mom said softly before leaving. Kyle nodded, offering her a reassuring smile, though he felt far from calm inside.

Now alone with Mr. Smith, Kyle sat down beside him on the bench. They sat in a quiet, shared understanding, both men lost in their thoughts. Kyle glanced at Autumn's dad, noticing how his shoulders drooped with exhaustion and sorrow. The night had taken a toll on him, and it was evident he hadn't eaten or rested in hours.

"Mr. Smith... would you like me to get you something to eat?" Kyle asked gently, hoping to offer a small comfort. "You can call me Smith," he replied, managing a faint smile. "And no, I'm alright. I don't feel much like eating."

Kyle nodded, but he couldn't shake the worry gnawing at him. He knew that going without food and rest wouldn't help anyone, especially in a time like this. After a few moments of silence, Kyle excused himself, heading outside to find a nearby shop. He returned a few minutes later with a couple of sandwiches, a bottle of water, and some tea, hoping it would be enough to encourage Mr. Smith to take a bite. "Here, Mr. Smith," Kyle said as he handed him a sandwich and tea. "Just a few bites. I think it'll help."

Mr. Smith hesitated, but after a moment, he accepted it. "Thank you, Kyle," he murmured, looking deeply appreciative. They sat together in silence, Mr. Smith finally taking small bites, his gaze unfocused as if lost in memories of Autumn. After a while, Mr. Smith turned to Kyle, his voice soft and a bit unsteady. “You know... I see why Autumn always spoke so highly of you. She really cared about you.” His words held a deep, quiet gratitude, and Kyle felt his heart ache as he thought of Autumn lying in the hospital bed.

Kyle managed a small, bittersweet smile. “She’s... she’s everything to me,” he said softly. “Meeting her changed everything.” He looked away, unable to hide the tears welling up in his eyes. Talking about her felt surreal, knowing she was just beyond that door, fighting to pull through. Mr. Smith glanced at him thoughtfully, a faint smile tugging at his lips despite the pain in his eyes. “You know, she used to be such a shy little thing. Always hiding behind her mother whenever strangers came around. But as she grew older, she became so warm, so kind to everyone she met.” He chuckled quietly, and his face softened as he recalled those memories.

Kyle listened intently, grateful for each glimpse into the life of the girl he adored. He could almost picture the young Autumn her father described—sweet, shy, and blossoming into the person he knew now. They talked quietly, exchanging memories of her, with Mr. Smith sharing stories of her childhood and Kyle recounting how they’d met. Eventually, Kyle noticed Mr. Smith’s eyes drooping with fatigue. “Maybe you should try to get some rest,” he suggested gently. “I’ll stay here and keep an eye on things.” Mr.

Smith hesitated but finally nodded, leaning back against the wall. Within minutes, he was asleep, his breathing soft and steady. Kyle sat beside him, keeping vigil over the quiet hall.

As the hours passed, Kyle's thoughts drifted back to his moments with Autumn. He remembered the way her laughter seemed to light up any space, how her eyes held a spark of kindness and mischief all at once. Every memory felt like a piece of a life he couldn't bear to lose. And yet, a knot of fear remained, twisting tighter with every silent minute that passed.

Kyle glanced at his phone, noting how the night had crept into the early hours of the morning. His mind was a chaotic storm of emotions—fear, hope, despair, and love—all swirling together in an endless loop. He thought of Autumn's laugh, her warmth, and her words. The quiet strength she had shown him so many times.

Despite the fear clawing at him, Kyle found himself whispering a silent prayer. He wasn't religious, but he believed that if anyone could hear him, maybe they'd understand just how much he needed her to be alright. He closed his eyes, his mind filled with memories and images of Autumn, hoping with every fiber of his being that she'd pull through. As dawn began to break, casting a pale light into the hallway, Kyle's resolve solidified. No matter what happened, he would be there for her.

He'd stay by her side, just as she had unknowingly stayed by his all this time, guiding him through even the smallest moments of doubt. Kyle looked over at Mr. Smith, who was still soundly asleep, and then back toward the room where Autumn lay. The light of a new day was beginning to seep into the hospital, signaling a fresh start, a hope that things could turn around. He just had to believe that she would be okay, that she'd wake up and smile at him again, that this nightmare would end with her pulling through, stronger than ever.

With the first light of morning filling the hallway, Kyle felt a sense of calm, fragile but real, settling over him. The waiting would continue, but so would his hope. He'd hold onto it for as long as it took. Kyle sat slumped on the uncomfortable waiting room chair, his head resting in his hands, every nerve in his body taut. He'd spent the night in silence, lost in thought, each tick of the clock dragging out the agony of not knowing what Autumn's fate would be. The sterile walls around him felt suffocating, the waiting endless.

Suddenly, a soft shuffling brought him out of his stupor, and he looked up to see a nurse approaching. She noticed Autumn's father, Mr. Smith, dozing fitfully in the chair beside him, and her face softened with understanding. “How are you holding up?” she asked Kyle gently, her voice a comforting murmur in the quiet hallway. Kyle forced a weak smile, the effort of it clear in the dark circles under his eyes. "I'm... I'm okay," he lied, though his worn-out posture and glassy eyes told a different story. Despite his words, he felt as if his heart was hanging on by a thread, ready to fray at the slightest whisper of bad news. The nurse gave him a nod, sympathy evident in her eyes. "The doctor will be here in about an hour," she said. "I know it's hard, but you should try to rest a bit before then. You've been up all night." Kyle nodded, though he knew that rest was an impossible idea. His mind was too restless, caught between worry and hope. "Thanks. I'll try," he said, giving her another faint smile, a polite gesture that masked the turmoil within.

Seeing his discomfort, the nurse hesitated, then added in a gentler tone, "She's stable for now, but... there may be some complications." The words hit Kyle like a punch to the gut. He felt his pulse quicken, a fresh wave of anxiety washing over him. He hadn't thought things could get worse, but the hint of ambiguity in her words was enough to send his mind spiraling. "Complications?" he echoed slowly.

The nurse's face softened, and she seemed to weigh her words carefully. "I'm afraid I can't say more. The doctor will explain everything in detail. But... it may be best to prepare yourself." Kyle's heart sank. He swallowed, feeling the ache of helplessness clawing at him. His gaze drifted toward the closed door behind which Autumn lay, fighting her own battle. The nurse offered him a small nod, then quietly walked away, leaving him once again alone with the weight of his thoughts. Unable to sit still, he decided to distract himself, if only temporarily. He gently got up, not wanting to disturb Mr. Smith, and made his way outside. The fresh morning air felt strangely grounding, even as the world outside seemed oblivious to his inner chaos. People were walking to work, children were laughing as they made their way to school, life going on as if nothing had changed. But for Kyle, everything felt different—every step felt heavier, every breath a reminder of how precarious things had become.

He found a small café nearby and ordered a couple of breakfast sandwiches and some coffee. Though he wasn't hungry, he knew he needed something to keep him going, to stay alert for whatever was to come. On his way back, he clutched the coffee cup, finding some comfort in its warmth. Small things—like the fresh morning air or the weight of the cup—felt like anchors, keeping him from drifting into despair. When he returned to the hospital, Mr. Smith was just waking up, his eyes red and weary as he looked around in confusion. Kyle approached him with a small smile, handing him the sandwich and coffee.

"Good morning, Mr. Smith," he said softly, careful not to startle him. Mr. Smith gave him a grateful nod, his voice rough with exhaustion. "Thank you, Kyle. You've been here all night..." Kyle offered a faint smile in response, though his thoughts were still clouded. "I spoke with the nurse," he said after a moment, choosing his words carefully. "She said Autumn's stable, but the doctor will come soon to explain. There might be... complications." Mr. Smith's face darkened, a new line of worry creasing his brow, though he nodded slowly, digesting the information. "I see... Thank you for letting me know, Kyle. Whatever happens, we'll face it together."

The two of them sat in silence, each lost in their thoughts. The sandwich and coffee provided a brief respite from the endless worry, a small moment of normalcy in the chaos. The act of sitting together, sharing a quiet breakfast, felt strangely comforting, as though they were both clinging to the little bits of life that still made sense. They were soon joined by Mrs. Smith and Kyle's mom, who had arrived, her face etched with concern. She immediately hugged Kyle, her embrace a balm to his frayed nerves. "Are you alright, honey?" she asked, gently brushing his hair out of his eyes.

Kyle nodded, though his face betrayed the exhaustion he felt. "I'm okay, Mom. I just... I just wish I knew she was going to be alright." As the morning hours stretched on, the waiting room gradually filled with the soft, anxious murmurs of Kyle, his mom, and Autumn's parents, each of them clinging to every bit of hope. Just as the first wave of sunlight filtered in, casting a gentle glow over the otherwise sterile space, the nurse returned with the doctor, his expression steady but serious as he approached the group. "Mr. and Mrs. Smith," the doctor began, nodding toward Autumn's parents, who immediately rose from their seats. Kyle leaned forward, every fiber of his being straining to catch each word.

The doctor gave a small nod. "First, let me tell you that Autumn is stable. She pulled through the night, and we're optimistic that she'll regain consciousness tomorrow." A wave of relief swept through them. Autumn's mom covered her mouth, visibly shaken yet visibly relieved, while Mr. Smith let out a breath he seemed to have been holding for hours. Kyle closed his eyes for a moment, feeling his own chest loosen, as if he'd just been granted permission to breathe again.

"However," the doctor continued, his tone turning more grave, "due to the nature of her injuries, this facility may not be fully equipped to handle her recovery. She will need to be transferred to a specialty hospital with advanced neuro-rehabilitation facilities as soon as possible." The words sank into him. The notion of Autumn being moved away, out of their immediate reach, added a new layer of worry. Autumn's parents exchanged uncertain glances, the reality settling in with weight. Kyle's heart sank at the thought—he had been holding on to the hope that she'd be close, that he could be there with her every step of the way. Mr. Smith cleared his throat, his voice rough but steady. "And... what about her condition? Once she's transferred, will she... will she make a full recovery?"

The doctor's face softened as he weighed his response carefully. "There's reason to be hopeful, but I must prepare you. The injury to her brain was severe. Given the trauma, there is a possibility that she may experience some memory loss, which could range from temporary lapses to permanent gaps. It's impossible to predict with certainty until she regains full consciousness and we can conduct further assessments." Kyle felt his stomach drop, a cold sense of dread seeping into his bones. The idea of Autumn waking up without her memories—perhaps even without remembering him or their moments together—felt unbearable. Memories were the threads that bound their relationship, the little glances, shared laughter, and quiet conversations beneath the stars. How could he imagine a life with her that was devoid of those connections? Mrs. Smith's voice was barely a whisper as she clutched her husband's arm. "Do you mean... she might not remember us?"

"It's a possibility," the doctor replied gently. "The brain is incredibly resilient, but trauma of this kind can have unpredictable effects. The good news is that there are treatments and therapies available to aid in recovery. With the right support and rehabilitation, there's hope." Kyle felt his breath catch. Hope. It was a fragile word, but he held onto it tightly. He could see the fear in Autumn's parents' eyes, a mixture of relief and fresh worry, as they processed the news. They nodded, thanking the doctor with wavering voices before he left them to consider the next steps.

As they settled back into their seats, Kyle's mom gently rubbed his back, sensing the weight of his thoughts. "She'll need you, Kyle," she whispered. "No matter what happens, you'll be there for her, right?"
Kyle nodded, steeling himself. "Yeah... of course, Mom."

After a moment, he turned to Mr. and Mrs. Smith, the determination clear in his voice. "If she needs to go to a different hospital, I'll visit her as often as I can. I'll do anything to help her get better. Even if..." he hesitated, "even if she doesn't remember me, I'll still be there."
Mrs. Smith reached over, placing a hand on his, her face soft with gratitude. "Thank you, Kyle. She's lucky to have someone like you." Kyle glanced down, his emotions swirling in ways he couldn't fully articulate. "I just want her to be okay," he said quietly.

With a newfound resolve, Kyle made a quick call to the rest of his friends, informing them of Autumn's condition and the doctor's plans for her transfer. The news struck them hard; their voices, usually filled with humor and energy, sounded unusually solemn on the phone. Each of them promised to be there for Kyle and for Autumn, no matter what it took. The doctor continued Based on her condition, I strongly recommend she be transferred to a facility outside the country." He paused, letting the gravity of his words settle over them. "I have a colleague—a renowned neurologist who specializes in trauma cases like Autumn's—and I believe she would have the best chance with his team."

The Smiths exchanged a worried glance evident on their faces. "Is there no other option, doctor?" Mrs. Smith asked, her voice barely audible. The doctor shook his head, sympathy in his eyes. "With the damage she's sustained, there's a possibility of complications, including memory loss. This facility offers specialized therapies and rehabilitation that could make all the difference in her recovery. It would mean several months away, perhaps longer, but it would give her the best chance." He looked at Kyle, who was staring at the floor, his hands clenched. "I know this is a lot to take in, but it's important to consider what's best for Autumn."

Kyle sat in the waiting room, feeling like the walls were closing in around him. The doctor's words echoed in his mind: "A facility outside the country... months of recovery... she might never be back." Each phrase felt like a hammer striking down on the hope he'd barely managed to cling to. Kyle's heart sank lower with each passing second. This wasn't how he had imagined things would go. He had always held on to the idea that once Autumn regained consciousness, things would slowly return to normal—that he'd be there for her, helping her through every step. But now, he was being faced with the possibility that she might be gone, out of reach, for an indefinite amount of time. Across from him, Mr. and Mrs. Smith sat in heavy contemplation, exchanging glances and holding each other's hands tightly. They could sense Kyle's pain and confusion, but they also had to think about what was best for their daughter. After a few minutes, Mr. Smith took a deep breath and looked at his wife, who nodded in silent agreement.

"We need to do whatever it takes to give her the best chance," Mr. Smith finally said. "The doctor's recommendation might be the best option." He turned to Kyle, his expression softening when he saw the look on the young man's face. "Kyle... I know this is hard. I wish things could be different. But this doctor overseas, he's one of the best, and Autumn's chances will be stronger under his care."

Kyle nodded, though the movement felt hollow. He struggled to keep his emotions in check, not wanting to break down in front of them. Autumn's parents were doing what any parent would—they were fighting for her life, and he couldn't fault them for it. Yet the thought of losing her, even temporarily, was unbearable. Mrs. Smith reached out, her hand gentle on his arm. "Kyle, I know how much you mean to her. And how much she means to you. This isn't goodbye forever." Her voice was soft but filled with sorrow, as though she were speaking not just to him but to herself as well. "She'll come back to us one day, and she'll need you more than ever when she does."

Kyle swallowed, his throat tight with the surge of emotions he was trying to suppress. "Thank you, Mrs. Smith," he whispered, his voice barely audible. "I just... I just don't know how I'm supposed to..." His words trailed off, and he couldn't bring himself to finish the sentence.

Sensing his need for space, Kyle's mom gently placed a hand on his shoulder. "Why don't you take a moment outside, sweetheart?" she suggested softly. "Get some fresh air." She turned to Autumn's parents with a reassuring smile. "I'll stay with him, don't worry."

Nodding, Kyle managed a quick, "Excuse me," before standing up and making his way out of the room, the weight of the situation pressing down on him with each step. Once outside, he leaned against thc cool wall of the hospital's exterior, letting the fresh air fill his lungs. He tilted his head back, looking up at the sky, his vision blurring as tears threatened to spill over. The thought of Autumn leaving, of her being across the world where he couldn't reach her, was more than he could bear. Kyle pressed his hands to his face, rubbing his temples as if he could force the pain to dissolve. He took a deep breath, trying to ground himself, but every time he closed his eyes, he saw Autumn's face, smiling at him, laughing with him. Every moment they'd shared felt like it was slipping away, as though someone was erasing her from his life with every second that passed.

After a few minutes, he heard the door open and felt a gentle touch on his shoulder. It was his mom, her face lined with concern as she wrapped an arm around him, pulling him close. "I know this isn't easy, honey," she said softly. "But you'll get through it. Autumn needs to get better, and this is her best chance. That's what matters most." Kyle nodded, his jaw clenched, trying to summon the strength he knew he'd need to face this reality. "I just... I thought we'd have time. I thought I'd be there to help her through this."

"I know," she murmured, rubbing his back in a soothing rhythm. "But think about it this way—this is a new beginning for her, a chance to heal. And when she comes back, she'll be stronger. You'll have your chance, Kyle. You just have to hold on a little while longer." He took a shaky breath and straightened up, wiping his face. "I guess I'll have to," he said, more to himself than to his mom.

After composing himself, Kyle walked back into the hospital, ready to face whatever came next. He found Mr. Smith on the phone, arranging the logistics of the transfer, speaking with a calm efficiency that belied the emotional weight of the moment. Mrs. Smith approached him as he came in, her expression filled with empathy and gratitude. "Thank you, Kyle, for being here with us," she said softly, her voice thick with emotion. "Autumn is lucky to have someone like you." Kyle nodded, managing a small smile. "I wouldn't be anywhere else." A few hours passed as they finalized the arrangements, and eventually, the nurse returned with the paperwork for the transfer. Mr. Smith spoke to Kyle, telling him that he could visit Autumn the following day before they began preparations to leave. Kyle's heart sank at the thought of saying goodbye, but he forced himself to remain calm, knowing this was about Autumn's recovery above all else. Later that day Kyle and Mr smith left home to get some rest, while Kyle's mom and Mrs smith stayed at the hospital.

The drive back to Kyle's house was saturated with a quiet, heart-wrenching tension. Mr. Smith's hands were steady on the steering wheel, but his gaze remained fixed on the road, as if searching for the right words to fill the silence. Kyle sat beside him, his thoughts lost in the reality he had yet to fully process—Autumn would be leaving, perhaps forever. He kept his face turned toward the window, watching the world blur past in muted colors as if it, too, were mourning with him.

As they neared Kyle's house, Mr. Smith broke the silence, his voice careful and soft. "Kyle, I need to be honest with you about what this means." He took a deep breath. "This isn't just about the treatment. It's a permanent move. My job is relocating permanently, and I'll be taking my family with me." Kyle swallowed hard, feeling his chest constrict. He had known, somewhere deep down, that this was coming. He had sensed it from the way Mr. Smith had spoken before, but hearing the words out loud made it real. Kyle's throat tightened, and he struggled to keep his voice steady. "I understand, Mr. Smith. Autumn's health... it has to come first."

The car slowed, and Mr. Smith pulled over to the side of the road, turning to look at Kyle with a sympathy that made Kyle's resolve tremble. Reaching out, Mr. Smith placed a hand on Kyle's shoulder, and his voice softened. "I don't think I'll ever be able to thank you enough for what you've done, Kyle. You've been there for Autumn in a way that not everyone would have. Kyle felt his composure falter. He fought to keep his emotions in check, to hold back the overwhelming sadness threatening to spill over. "There's no need to thank me," he managed, his voice barely a whisper. "I just... I just want her to be happy and healthy. I'll be okay with that, even if..." He hesitated, the words lodging painfully in his throat. "Even if she won't remember me."

"You're a good man, Kyle. I can see why Autumn cared for you so much. I only hope... I only hope life brings you two together again someday." Kyle felt the weight of those words settle heavily within him. Deep down, he knew the chances of that were slim—Autumn would soon be leaving, and her life would change in ways he couldn't begin to fathom. But he mustered a faint smile, nodding as if those words held a promise, he could somehow believe in. "Thank you, Mr. Smith," he replied, his voice steady despite the ache in his heart.

Back at home, the hours passed in a blur. Kyle moved through the day as though he were trapped in a fog, the world around him fading into the background. He tried to distract himself by doing small tasks around the house, but his mind kept drifting back to Autumn. The idea that she would soon be gone, out of his life and perhaps out of his memory, left him feeling as if he were losing a part of himself. Night came and went, with sleep eluding him as he lay in bed, staring up at the ceiling, his mind replaying every moment they'd shared together. When morning finally arrived, it brought with it a strange sense of calm, a quiet acceptance that settled over him like a fragile peace. Today, he would see Autumn one last time, even if she couldn't respond, even if all he could do was sit by her side and say goodbye in his heart.

The next morning arrived faster than he was ready for, and he quickly dressed and headed out the door to meet Mr. Smith. The drive to the hospital felt heavy, neither of them speaking much, both lost in their own thoughts. As they walked through the hospital's sterile hallways, the quiet tension grew, each step bringing Kyle closer to a moment he dreaded and longed for all at once.

They reached the waiting room where Kyle's mom and Mrs. Smith were sitting. Mrs. Smith's face brightened slightly when she saw them, a hopeful glimmer in her eyes. She rose to greet them, brushing her hands nervously against her coat as she smiled faintly. "The doctor says we'll be able to see her today. She might be conscious, even if only for a little while. She won't be able to speak, but... she should be able to hear us." A wave of relief and sadness hit Kyle all at once. He would get to be near her again, to tell her everything he wanted her to know, even if she couldn't respond. It was a small comfort, but it felt like the most precious thing in the world to him now. He took a seat beside Mrs. Smith, both of them waiting in a shared silence, united in the tension and anticipation.

Kyle's mom reached out to squeeze his hand, her expression one of quiet strength. She had been there for him since the accident, her presence a comforting anchor amid the chaos of emotions that had flooded his life. Kyle looked at her gratefully, and she nodded back, her face filled with unspoken support. He knew she understood what this moment meant to him. Minutes stretched into what felt like hours, each passing second laden with a mixture of dread and hope. The hospital felt almost like a world of its own, each hallway whispering the quiet, unyielding routine of care and recovery. Nurses moved about quietly, occasionally glancing at the small group waiting outside Autumn's room. Mrs. Smith's excitement was almost palpable, a fragile hope in her eyes as she held onto the thought of seeing her daughter conscious, even if only for a short time. Kyle could sense her nervous energy, her hands wringing together as she looked toward the closed door of Autumn's room, waiting for the signal that they could go in.

A nurse stepped out of the room, glancing around before her eyes met theirs. "It won't be long now," she said softly, her gaze lingering on each of them. The sincerity in her voice reassured them, giving them a small glimmer of hope to hold onto. She glanced at Mrs. Smith, then at Kyle, before continuing on her rounds, her quiet demeanor comforting in the midst of their turmoil. Kyle sat back, drawing in a steadying breath. His mind was a swirl of emotions, his heart racing as he thought about the reality of seeing Autumn awake. Even if she couldn't speak, even if it was only for a few moments, he was ready to pour his heart out to her, to tell her all the things he couldn't before. The minutes stretched on. The doctor's words lingered in Kyle's mind: she would regain consciousness, but there was no guarantee of how much she'd remember or

what complications might arise. It was a bittersweet hope, and as Kyle sat beside her family, he resolved to make the most of the time he'd have with her.
As the first light of morning began to filter through the hospital windows, casting a gentle glow over the waiting area, everyone held their breath, knowing that the moment they'd waited for was drawing near. They just needed to wait a little longer, to hold on to hope a little tighter.

Every second felt like an eternity, his thoughts a storm of hope and fear. When the nurse finally stepped out of Autumn's room, her calm expression brought a wave of relief to the group. "You can speak to her," she said gently, her voice barely above a whisper. "But only one at a time."

Autumn's mom stood immediately, her hands trembling slightly as she straightened her blouse. Without a word, she walked toward the door, pausing just briefly to compose herself before stepping inside. The door clicked softly behind her, leaving the rest of them waiting in silence. Kyle sat on the edge of his seat, his gaze fixed on the door. His palms were clammy, and his mind raced with the things he wanted to say to Autumn, but he struggled to piece his emotions into coherent thoughts. He clenched his fists, trying to stay calm, but the sheer weight of the situation was suffocating.

After about 15 minutes, the door opened again, and Mrs. Smith emerged, her face a mixture of relief and joy. She dabbed at her eyes with a tissue, her voice trembling with emotion as she spoke. "She... she twitched her eyes and hands," she said, her smile faint but genuine.

Kyle exhaled, his chest loosening just slightly at the news. Mrs. Smith looked at her husband, nodding for him to go next. Mr. Smith stood, his typically composed demeanor softening as he walked toward the door. While he was inside, Kyle's mind raced even faster. What will I say to her? he wondered, over and over again. He thought of all the conversations they'd shared, all the times they'd laughed together. The reality of her lying in that hospital bed, hurt and fragile, was something he wasn't ready for.

When Mr. Smith returned, there was a noticeable change in his expression. He looked more confident, more at peace. "She's going to be okay," he said simply, his voice carrying a quiet strength. "She's still fighting, and I know she'll make it through." Kyle swallowed hard, his throat dry. Mr. Smith gave him an encouraging nod. "It's your turn, son."

Kyle stood, his legs feeling shaky as he made his way to the door. He paused for a moment, his hand on the handle, taking a deep breath to steady himself before he opened it. The room was quiet, save for the rhythmic beeping of the machines monitoring Autumn's vitals. There she was, lying in the hospital bed, her head wrapped in white bandages, her face pale but still so familiar. Kyle's chest tightened at the sight. Her frailty was heartbreaking, a stark contrast to the vibrant, lively person he knew.

He walked slowly to her bedside, pulling a chair closer before sitting down. He stared at her for a moment, unable to stop the tears welling up in his eyes. Reaching out, he brushed a stray strand of hair from her forehead, his touch gentle and hesitant. "Why did this happen, Autumn?" he whispered, his voice breaking. "You didn't deserve this." Tears began to fall freely now, and he didn't bother wiping them away. "I... I can't bear to see you like this," he said softly, his hand trembling as he reached for hers. Her fingers felt cool in his grasp, but he held on tightly, as though afraid to let go.

"I love you, Autumn," he whispered, his voice cracking under the pressure of his emotions. "I love you so much. Please, please get well soon."

As he sat there, he suddenly felt a faint squeeze against his hand. His breath hitched, his heart leaping at the small sign of response. "Autumn?" he asked, his voice barely audible. The squeeze was weak but unmistakable. Relief flooded through him, and he smiled through his tears. "You're still fighting, aren't you?" he said, his voice trembling with hope. "Promise me you'll get better, Autumn. Promise me you'll come back to us."

The room remained silent, save for the sound of her breathing and the steady beeping of the machines. Kyle wiped his face with his sleeve, trying to compose himself, but the tears wouldn't stop. "They told me... they told me you might lose some memories," he said, his voice faltering. "You might forget me. Forget us."

He lowered his head, his tears falling onto her hand. "But even if you do... even if you don't remember me, I'll still be here for you, Autumn. I'll always be here."

For a long while, Kyle just sat there, holding her hand, his thumb gently stroking her fingers. The silence between them was heavy, but it was filled with unspoken words, emotions he couldn't fully express. He tried to commit every detail of her face to memory—the curve of her cheek, the way her lashes rested against her skin, the soft rise and fall of her chest. Finally, he knew it was time. His time with her was up, and he needed to gather the strength to say goodbye, even if it wasn't forever. He took a deep breath, squeezing her hand one last time. "I'll always love you, Autumn," he whispered. "No matter what happens." With every ounce of courage he could muster, Kyle stood and walked to the door. He glanced back once, taking in the sight of her before stepping outside, the weight of the moment pressing heavily on his shoulders.

Kyle walked out of the hospital, each step heavier than the last, the air around him thick with despair. He had just seen Autumn lying in that bed, surrounded by machines, fragile and unresponsive. The image haunted him as he headed straight home. His chest ached with emotions he couldn't process, and his thoughts swirled with frustration, disbelief, and sadness. He barely noticed when he arrived home, brushing past his mom's concerned voice calling after him. Locking himself in his room, he sank onto his bed and stared at the ceiling. The silence of his room was suffocating, amplifying the thoughts in his head. For hours, he replayed the last few days in his mind—the accident, the hospital, the doctor's words about Autumn's future.

How could everything fall apart so suddenly? Just days ago, they were together, laughing and sharing dreams, and now she was slipping away from him, piece by piece. The next morning came quickly. Kyle barely slept, but the loud blaring of his alarm reminded him that it was game day. The school's football team had a big match, and while it should've excited him, Kyle felt nothing. He went through the motions of getting ready, lacing his cleats, and heading to the field, but his mind remained elsewhere.

When the whistle blew to start the game, Kyle snapped into action, channeling his frustration into every kick, every sprint, and every tackle. His movements were sharp, calculated, and unrelenting, as though he could outrun the pain coursing through him. By halftime, the team led 3-0, thanks largely to Kyle's performance. By the end, they had secured a dominating 5-0 victory. But even as the crowd cheered and his teammates celebrated, Kyle didn't feel victorious.

"Kyle, man, you killed it out there!" Ryan called, jogging over and slapping him on the back. "You were unstoppable," Ryder added, his tone a mix of awe and encouragement.

Kyle simply nodded; his expression distant. He barely muttered a "thanks" before walking away. "Come on, dude," Sam chimed in, trying to lighten the mood. "We're heading to the diner. You've earned a mountain of fries and a shake."

"I'm not hungry," Kyle said flatly, brushing past them. His friends exchanged worried glances, but they knew better than to push him. Kyle wasn't himself, and they understood why.

The days that followed passed in a blur. Kyle went through his daily routine, but his heart wasn't in anything. Every moment felt like an eternity as he counted down to the day Autumn would leave. He tried to convince himself he would be okay, but the thought of never seeing her again was unbearable. Finally, the dreaded day arrived. Kyle woke early, unable to sleep any longer, the weight of the morning pressing heavily on him. His mom, sensing his turmoil, silently prepared to go with him. She didn't ask questions, knowing he needed space to process everything. The drive to Autumn's house was quiet. Kyle stared out the window, his mind racing. When they arrived, they saw Autumn's parents busy packing their belongings into a trailer. Mr. Smith greeted them with a warm but weary smile. "Kyle, thank you for coming," he said, patting Kyle on the back.

Kyle nodded, swallowing hard. "Of course," he managed, his voice barely.

Without waiting for further instruction, Kyle set to work, lifting boxes and helping Mr. Smith load them into the trailer. The physical effort was a welcome distraction, giving him something to focus on other than the ache in his chest. Each box he carried felt heavier than it should—not because of its physical weight but because of what it symbolized. Every item packed away was another piece of Autumn's life being moved far beyond his reach. For an hour, Kyle worked tirelessly alongside Mr. Smith, barely exchanging words. The silence between them was heavy but not uncomfortable. Mr. Smith occasionally glanced at Kyle, his face etched with gratitude and sadness. When the last box was loaded into the trailer, Mr. Smith sighed deeply. "Thank you, Kyle," he said softly.

Kyle gave a small nod, brushing the sweat from his forehead. "It's the least I can do," he replied, though his voice cracked slightly. Mr. Smith looked at him, his expression a mixture of admiration and sorrow. "We're planning to move Autumn in a few hours. You should pay her a visit at the hospital before then," he said.

Kyle froze for a moment, the words hitting him like a blow. He'd known this moment was coming, but hearing it said aloud made it all too real. Gathering his courage, he nodded.
"I'll go," he said.

Kyle stayed a little longer, helping secure the last few boxes and tidying up the area. When he and his mom finally headed to the hospital, the drive felt both agonizingly slow and far too quick. Kyle's mind raced with thoughts of what he would say to Autumn, though he knew no words would ever feel enough.

As they arrived at the hospital, Kyle saw a scene he hadn't prepared himself for. Autumn was being wheeled out of the hospital, surrounded by medical staff and her parents. The sight of her, still fragile and connected to machines, tore at his heart. He couldn't move at first, his legs frozen as he watched the orderly guide her toward the ambulance waiting outside. His mom placed a gentle hand on his shoulder, grounding him enough to take a hesitant step forward. Autumn's parents noticed him and approached. Mrs. Smith's face was a mix of exhaustion and hope. She reached out and held his hand briefly.

"Thank you for everything," she said, her voice trembling.
"I... I just want her to be okay," Kyle said, his voice barely audible. Mr. Smith stepped forward, pulling a folded piece of paper from his pocket. "Autumn wrote this," he said, handing the letter to Kyle. "She wrote it the day before the accident. We found it among her things." Kyle stared at the letter in his hands, his vision blurring as tears welled up. He wanted to read it immediately, but his emotions were too raw to focus. Instead, he clutched it tightly, nodding in silent gratitude. "We'll take good care of her," Mr. Smith said, his tone gentle but firm. Kyle's throat felt dry, and his chest ached as he watched Autumn's stretcher being loaded into the ambulance. She was so close, yet so far, and every moment felt like it was slipping through his fingers.

The ambulance doors closed with a soft click, and the vehicle began to pull away. Kyle stood there, unable to move, his eyes fixed on it as it disappeared down the road. He felt like the world had shifted beneath him, leaving him unmoored. As the sound of the ambulance faded, Kyle remained rooted to the spot, clutching the letter tightly. His mom called his name softly, but he couldn't respond. There was no pain greater than what he felt in that moment—the pain of knowing he might never see Autumn again.

Kyle told his mom that he needed to go somewhere and asked her to head home. "Don't worry about me, okay?" he said, forcing a weak smile. She nodded hesitantly, sensing the weight he carried, but trusted him enough to let him go. He started his bike, and the engine roared louder than usual, cutting through the stillness of his mind. The streets blurred past him, but his focus wasn't on the road—it was on the envelope tucked safely in his jacket pocket. His hands gripped the handlebars tightly, the cool wind biting at his face. Kyle had never ridden his bike so fast before, and yet it felt like he couldn't reach his destination soon enough.

The treehouse was waiting for him, a place that held the echoes of laughter, secrets, and memories of times when life was simpler. When he arrived, he parked his bike hastily and stood there for a moment, staring at the old wooden structure as if it were calling to him.

Kyle climbed up the sturdy ladder, each step bringing back a memory of the times he and his friends had spent here. But this time, the weight on his shoulders made the climb feel heavier. When he finally reached the top and stepped inside, everything looked just as it always had—the cozy, worn sofa, the shelves lined with trinkets they'd collected, and the faint smell of wood and dust. He sat down on the sofa, sinking into it as though it could absorb all the emotions threatening to spill out. The letter trembled in his hands, its presence both comforting and terrifying. He ran his thumb over the edges of the envelope, debating whether to open it. A part of him didn't want to know what it said, afraid of what emotions it might unleash.

Kyle set the letter down on the small table in front of him and leaned back, closing his eyes. That's when he noticed something out of the corner of his eye. Lying on the armrest of the sofa was a scarf—a familiar, vibrant one. His chest tightened as he picked it up, the fabric soft and slightly faded from use. It was Autumn's scarf.

He remembered the day she brought it with her, draping it over her shoulders as he showed her around the treehouse for the first time. Her laughter echoed in his mind, clear as day. She had marveled at the place, running her fingers over the worn furniture and admiring the view from the window.

Kyle held the scarf to his chest like it was the last piece of her he had left. He squeezed it tightly, his fingers trembling. Every corner of this treehouse reminded him of her, but this small, tangible piece of her felt like it was keeping him grounded. Time passed slowly as Kyle sat there, the silence of the treehouse broken only by the occasional rustle of leaves outside. He stared out the window, the view as breathtaking as ever—the endless expanse of green, dotted with hints of orange from the trees. Autumn had stood at this very spot, her eyes lighting up at the beauty of the scenery.

Kyle stood by the window now, placing his hands on the sill, his mind flooded with memories. He could almost feel her standing beside him, her shoulder brushing against his. He closed his eyes, wishing he could go back to that moment, to a time when she was right there with him. Eventually, his gaze returned to the letter on the table. He couldn't avoid it any longer. With a deep breath, he walked over, sat down, and picked it up again. His hands shook as he tore open the envelope carefully, almost reverently. The paper inside was neatly folded, and as he opened it, he immediately recognized Autumn's handwriting—small and precise, yet warm, just like her. He hesitated for a moment before beginning to read.

Dear Kyle,

If you're holding this letter, it means something has changed—something neither of us could have predicted or controlled. Writing this feels like leaving a piece of my soul behind, and yet, it's the only way I can make sure you know everything I've been carrying in my heart. Kyle, you are the best thing that has ever happened to me. You saw me when I couldn't even see myself. You loved me when I didn't feel worthy of love. You believed in me when I was too scared to believe in myself. Do you know how rare that is? To find someone who looks at you, broken pieces and all, and still thinks you're worth the world?

You've given me more than I could have ever asked for. You made me laugh on days I wanted to cry, and you reminded me that it's okay to be human—to stumble, to fall, and to rise again. I'll never forget the moments we've shared: the quiet conversations, the stolen glances, the times when we didn't need words to understand each other. Those memories are mine to keep forever, no matter where life takes us.

Kyle, do you remember the portrait you drew of me? I never got to tell you how much I loved it. You captured something in me I never saw in myself. The way you sketched my smile, as if it was something so full of life and light, made me feel like maybe I could be that person after all. I kept staring at it, wondering how someone could see me in a way I didn't even see myself. It's one of the most beautiful gifts I've ever received, and I'll carry the memory of it with me always.

But life, as it always does, has a way of pulling people apart. If I'm not with you right now, I need you to promise me something. Promise me you'll keep living. Not just existing, but truly living. Find joy in the little things, chase the dreams you've told me about, and never let the weight of the past hold you down.

You've got a heart so full of kindness, Kyle, and the world desperately needs people like you.I don't know what my future holds, but I know yours is going to be bright. You have so much to offer, so much love to give, and so many stories left to write. And Kyle, you've taught me what it means to love selflessly.

I want you to know that even if I'm far away, even if memories fade, you'll always be a part of me. You've left an imprint on my soul that time can never erase.

I love you, Kyle. I've loved you in ways I didn't know I could, and I'll keep loving you no matter what happens.

And one last thing: I know you're writing a book—one of your dreams I hope you never give up on. I hope, in some small way, that the pages of that book hold a little bit of me. A memory, a moment, a feeling—anything that keeps us alive in the words you write.

Yours always,
Autumn

Kyle sat in the treehouse, the crumpled letter trembling in his hands as the last words echoed in his mind: "I hope some of the pages of the book are about me." He whispered to himself, his voice breaking, "A few pages about you? My dear, this whole book is about you."

Tears spilled over despite his efforts to hold them back. Autumn's words lingered like a ghost in the room, filling the silence with an aching weight he couldn't escape. He clutched her scarf tighter against his chest, feeling its softness as if it were her touch, her presence. The pain in his heart felt immeasurable, an ache that no words could ever describe. He leaned against the wall of the treehouse, staring out at the world beyond the window. The golden hues of the setting sun painted the horizon, but its beauty only deepened his sadness. His chest heaved as he whispered to the emptiness, "Why did it have to be this way? Why her?" He shook his head and wiped his face.

But then, amidst the pain, a thought rose in his mind. Autumn wouldn't want this. She wouldn't want me to drown in sorrow. He exhaled deeply and sat up, wiping the tears from his cheeks with the back of his hand. He forced himself to take slow, deep breaths, trying to calm the storm inside him. Kyle clenched the scarf in one hand and laid the letter gently beside him on the sofa. He gazed out the window again, watching the leaves sway in the wind, their gentle rustling almost like a comforting whisper. But the grief was still there, heavy and relentless. He whispered to himself again, his voice cracking, "I wish I could go back to one of those nights where I fell asleep knowing I'd see you again." The days that followed blurred together. Kyle walked through them like a shadow, detached from everything around him. The classes he once enjoyed now felt lifeless, the chatter of his peers distant and hollow. He sat in his usual seat, surrounded by familiar faces, but their voices seemed muffled, drowned out by the emptiness he felt inside.

His friends tried to pull him out of his sorrow, their jokes and antics as lively as ever, but nothing seemed to reach him. Ryan's poorly-timed jokes, Nate's nerdy enthusiasm, and even Sam's sharp wit—all of it felt muted. Kyle forced himself to smile and laugh occasionally, but his heart wasn't in it. He would go home each day and sit in his room, staring at the scarf or rereading Autumn's letter, unable to move on. The pain lingered, but Kyle carried it quietly, just as he carried her memory. As weeks turned to months, the seasons changed, and life marched on relentlessly. Kyle threw himself into his studies, using them as a distraction. He spent hours at his desk, focusing on projects and exams, trying to keep his mind occupied. Yet, even in his quiet moments of productivity, Autumn's presence lingered—her laugh, her smile, the way her eyes lit up when she was happy.

When the final semester approached, Kyle realized how close he was to graduation. The thought filled him with an odd mix of relief and sorrow. This was supposed to be a milestone he celebrated with Autumn. She should have been there with him, teasing him about his nerves or encouraging him with her boundless support.

Finally, graduation day arrived. Kyle stood among his classmates, in the traditional robes, the cap perched awkwardly on his head. The ceremony was long, filled with speeches and applause, but it all passed in a haze. He looked out at the crowd, spotting his mom beaming proudly in the audience. His friends were beside him, excited and full of energy, but Kyle's heart felt heavy.

When his name was called, he stepped onto the stage, accepting his diploma with a forced smile. The applause was loud, but all he could think about was how much he wished Autumn could see him now. As he stepped off the stage, he whispered under his breath, "This one's for you, Autumn." After the ceremony, Kyle and his friends gathered for photos and final goodbyes. They reminisced about their time together, sharing memories of late-night study sessions, wild adventures, and everything in between. For a moment, Kyle allowed himself to smile genuinely. These friends had been his anchor, his lifeline during the hardest times.

Later that evening, Kyle found himself alone in the treehouse once more. The diploma rested on the table beside him, and Autumn's letter was still tucked safely in his bag. He stared out at the night sky, the stars twinkling faintly above.

"I did it, Autumn," he whispered. "I graduated. Just like we talked about." His voice wavered, and he closed his eyes, letting the silence surround him. Though the pain remained, there was also a quiet strength within him—a resolve to keep moving forward, even if it was without her by his side. And so, Kyle sat there, looking out at the endless expanse of stars, carrying her memory with him as he prepared to face whatever came next.

Years had passed, yet the memory of Autumn lingered in Kyle's heart like a warm yet painful ache. He had moved on with his life—or at least, he told himself he had. His friends kept him updated on everyone from their old days, and while he appreciated their efforts, he always felt a pang of longing when they mentioned her. One day, while sitting in his quiet apartment, his phone buzzed with a message from Ryan. "Guess what? Autumn is coming back to Orange for a few days!"

Kyle's heart stopped. He stared at the message, his chest tightening. She was coming back. But before he could let the thought settle, Ryan followed up with another message. "Oh, by the way, she's married now. And she has a kid!"

The words hit Kyle like a hammer. His heart shattered into pieces he thought he had long since repaired. He stared blankly at the screen, the message burning into his mind. He felt a swirl of emotions—pain, sadness, and an odd sense of relief knowing she was happy.

That night, Kyle sat alone, clutching a worn scarf that had once belonged to her. He whispered to himself, "You always wanted her to be happy. Now she is." He repeated those words like a mantra, trying to convince himself. But deep inside, a small voice cried out: You're not ready for this.

The day finally arrived. Kyle knew she was in town and decided he needed to see her. He didn't want to interrupt her life or disrupt her happiness. He just needed to see her smile again, even if it was from afar. Kyle found himself near the town square where he heard she would be. His heart raced as he scanned the crowd. And then he saw her. There she was, standing with her husband and their child. She looked radiant, her smile as bright as he remembered, maybe even brighter. Her laughter floated across the air, filling the space around her with warmth. Kyle's breath hitched in his throat.

For a long moment, he stood frozen, unable to move or tear his eyes away. He watched as her son ran around, laughing and playing, her husband standing beside her with an arm around her shoulders. The sight tore him apart. Yet, at the same time, a small part of him felt...happy. She deserved this joy, this life.

Kyle stayed rooted to the spot, watching them from a distance. He didn't want to approach her, didn't want to intrude on her happiness. He thought about all the moments they had shared, all the love he had held for her, and how that love now existed as a quiet part of him—still alive, but no longer loud.

As he turned to leave, his vision blurred by tears, he heard a voice call out, "Kyle, wait!"

His heart stopped. He froze in place, barely able to breathe. She had seen him. She had recognized him.

He turned slowly, his heart pounding in his chest. But then he realized she wasn't talking to him. She was calling her son. "Kyle!" she called again; her voice filled with affection. "Come back here!"

Her son laughed and ran back toward her, wrapping his small arms around her legs. The realization hit him like a wave. She had named her son Kyle. He didn't know whether to laugh or cry. Tears welled up in his eyes, and a bittersweet smile spread across his face. He whispered to himself, "Of all the names in the world..."

With one last glance at her, he turned away, unable to watch any longer. He walked briskly to his bike, climbed on, and rode off, the roar of the engine drowning out the sounds of the town. Kyle found himself at the orange tree, the place where he and Autumn had shared so many special moments. The sun was setting, painting the sky in hues of orange and gold, the colors reflecting the bittersweet memories in his heart.

He sat beneath the tree, his back leaning against its sturdy trunk. He pulled out his notebook, the one where he had poured out his thoughts and feelings over the years. For a while, he simply sat there, staring at the blank page before him. He thought about Autumn, about the love they had shared, and about how life had taken them on such different paths. He thought about the pain of losing her and the quiet acceptance he had tried to cultivate over the years. Finally, he picked up his pen and began to write. The words flowed from his heart, each one carrying a piece of his soul. He poured out everything he had felt—the joy, the sorrow, the love, and the heartbreak. He wrote about the moments they had shared, the promises they had made, and the dreams they had once had. And then, as the last rays of sunlight disappeared beyond the horizon, he wrote the final line.

“So, this is what love feels like...”

www.ingramcontent.com/pod-product-compliance
Lightning Source LLC
LaVergne TN
LVHW091313150826
845673LV00006B/1631